Get Ready for Pre-K

Jumbo Workbook

This workbook belongs to

....

Use pencils, crayons, and stickers to complete the activities in this book. When there is a sticker missing, you will see this pattern:

Dear Parents and Families,

Welcome to the *Get Ready for Pre-K Jumbo Workbook*!

Here are some tips to help ensure that your child gets the most from this book.

★ Look at the pages with your child, ensuring they know what to do before starting.

★ Plan short, regular sessions, doing only one or two pages at a time.

★ Praise your child's efforts and improvements.

★ Encourage your child to assess their own efforts in a positive way. For example, say: "You've drawn some great triangles there. Which one do you think you did best?"

★ Make the learning sessions positive experiences. Give prompts where they might help. If a section is too hard for your child, leave those pages until they are ready for them.

★ Relate the learning to things in your child's world. For example, if your child is working on a page about the color red, ask them to find some red things in your home.

★ There are stickers to use throughout the book. They help build your child's hand–eye coordination and observation skills. Encourage your child to place the stickers on each page before starting the other activities.

Together, the activities in the workbook help build a solid understanding of early learning concepts to ensure your child is ready for pre-k or preschool.

We wish your child hours of enjoyment with this fun workbook!

Scholastic Early Learning

Contents

Party fun

Trace the strings on the balloons.
Start at the big red dot.

Smart stripes

Trace the stripes on the boy's T-shirt.

Picture gallery

Trace the picture frames.

Rainbow kites

Trace the kites.

Starfish

Trace the starfish.

Birthday gift

Trace the gift.

The horse's stable

Trace the stable door.

Flower fun

Trace the petals on the flower.

Googly glasses

Trace the girl's toy glasses.

Lollipop!

Trace the spiral in the lollipop.

Wiggly snakes

Trace the snakes.

Lots of legs

Trace the octopus's legs.

Beautiful beads

Trace the pretty beads on the necklace.

Tasty watermelon

Trace the watermelon slices.

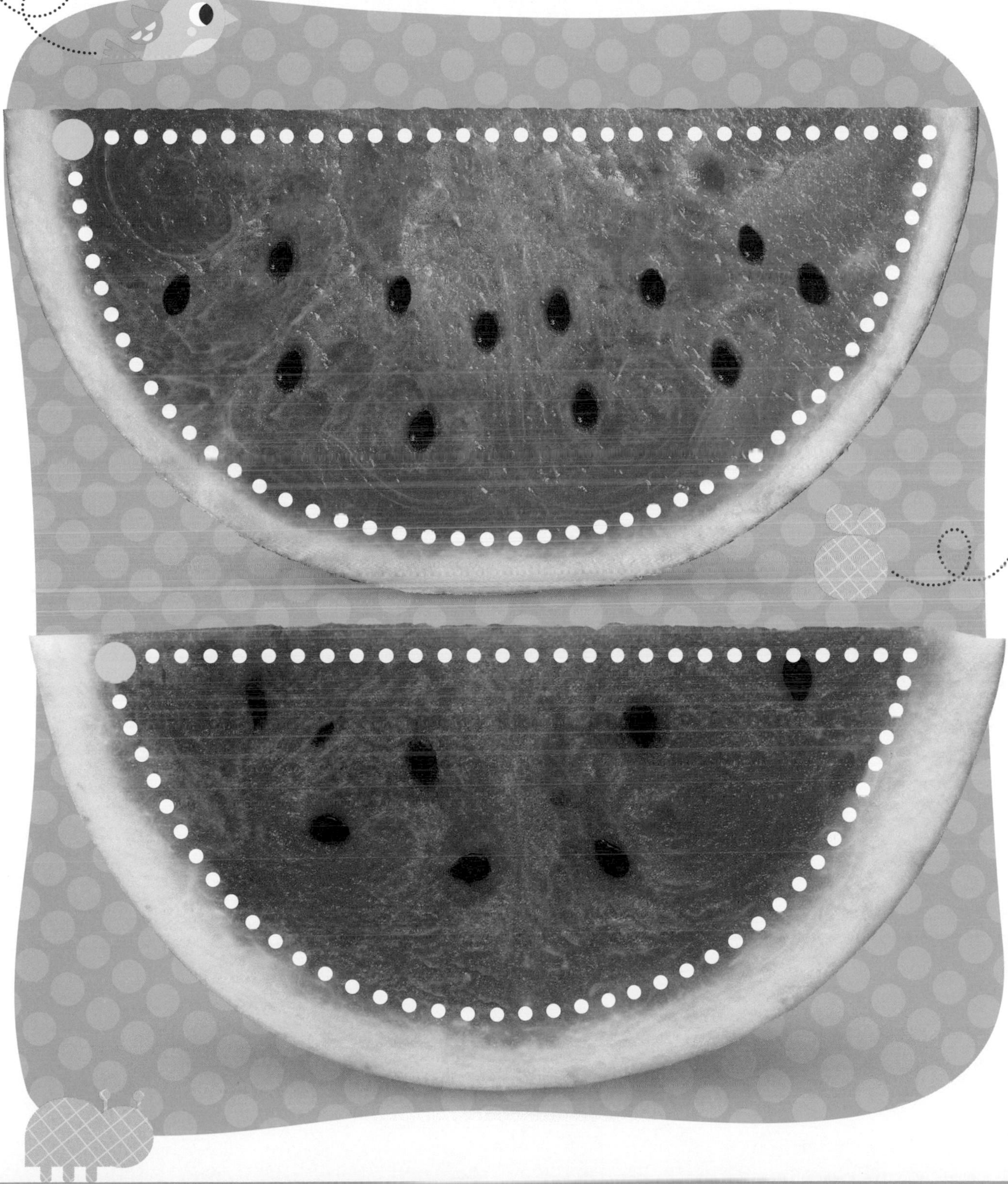

Cute cat

Trace the cat.

A cool car

Trace the car.

Lots of dots

Trace the ladybug.

Blast off!

Trace the rocket.

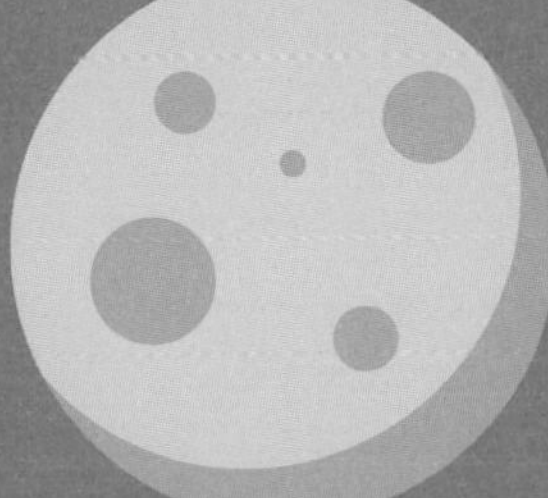

Five little ducks

Help the ducks reach the other side of the pond.

Start→

Finish

Bunny's burrow

Help the rabbit find its way back to its bunnies.

Start

Finish

Chirping chicks

Help the hen find her chicks.

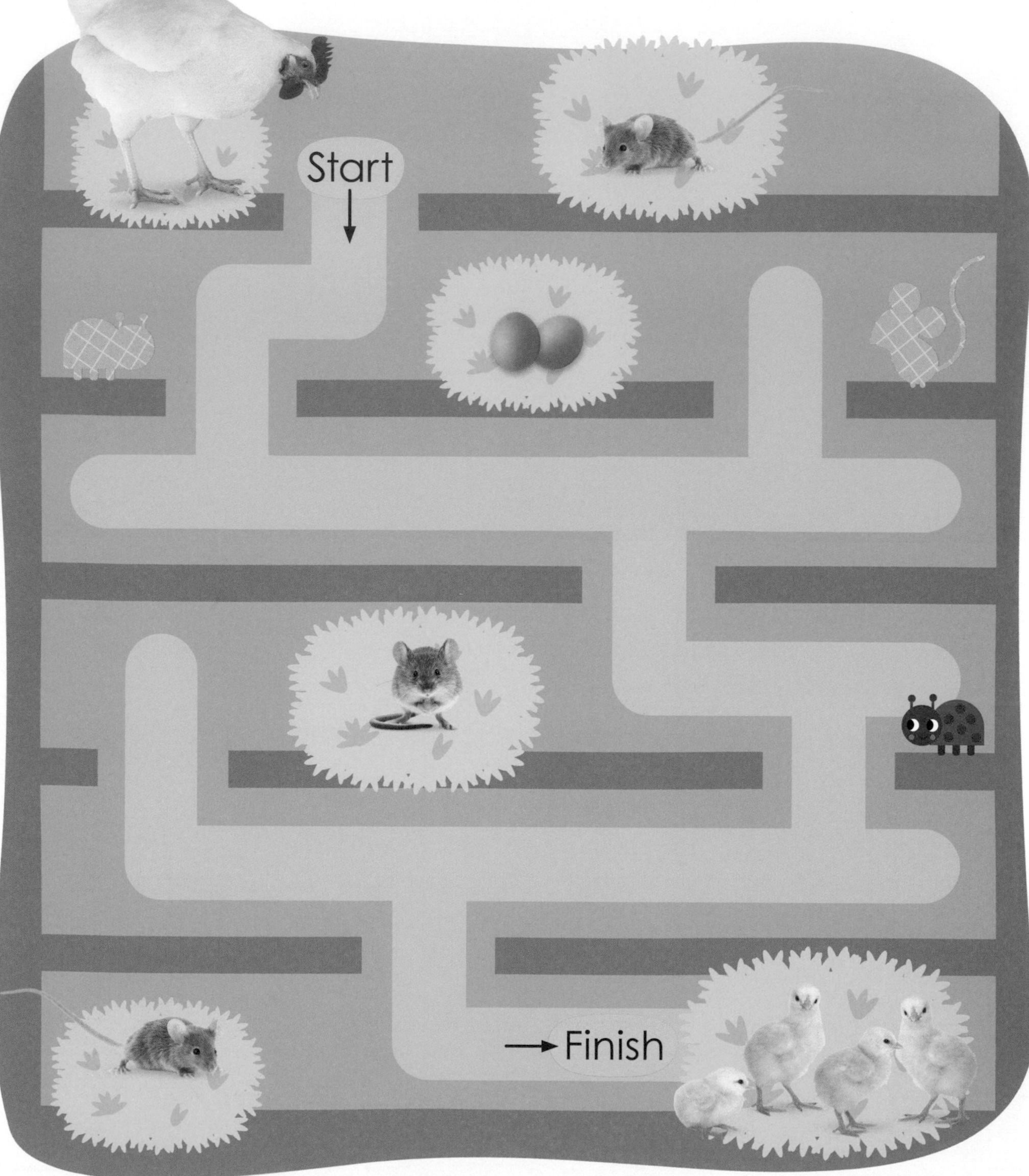

Car race

Help the race car reach the finish line.

Start →

→ Finish

Fun on the farm

Help the farmer find his tractor.

Web wander

Help the spider find its way through the web.

Start

Finish

Pig puzzle

Help the pig return to its pigsty.

Monkey business

Help the monkey reach the bananas.

Start →

Cheese, please!

Help the mouse find the cheese.

Start →

→ Finish

Teddy bear's picnic

Help the teddy bear find the picnic.

Fishy friends

Help the fish swim to its friend.

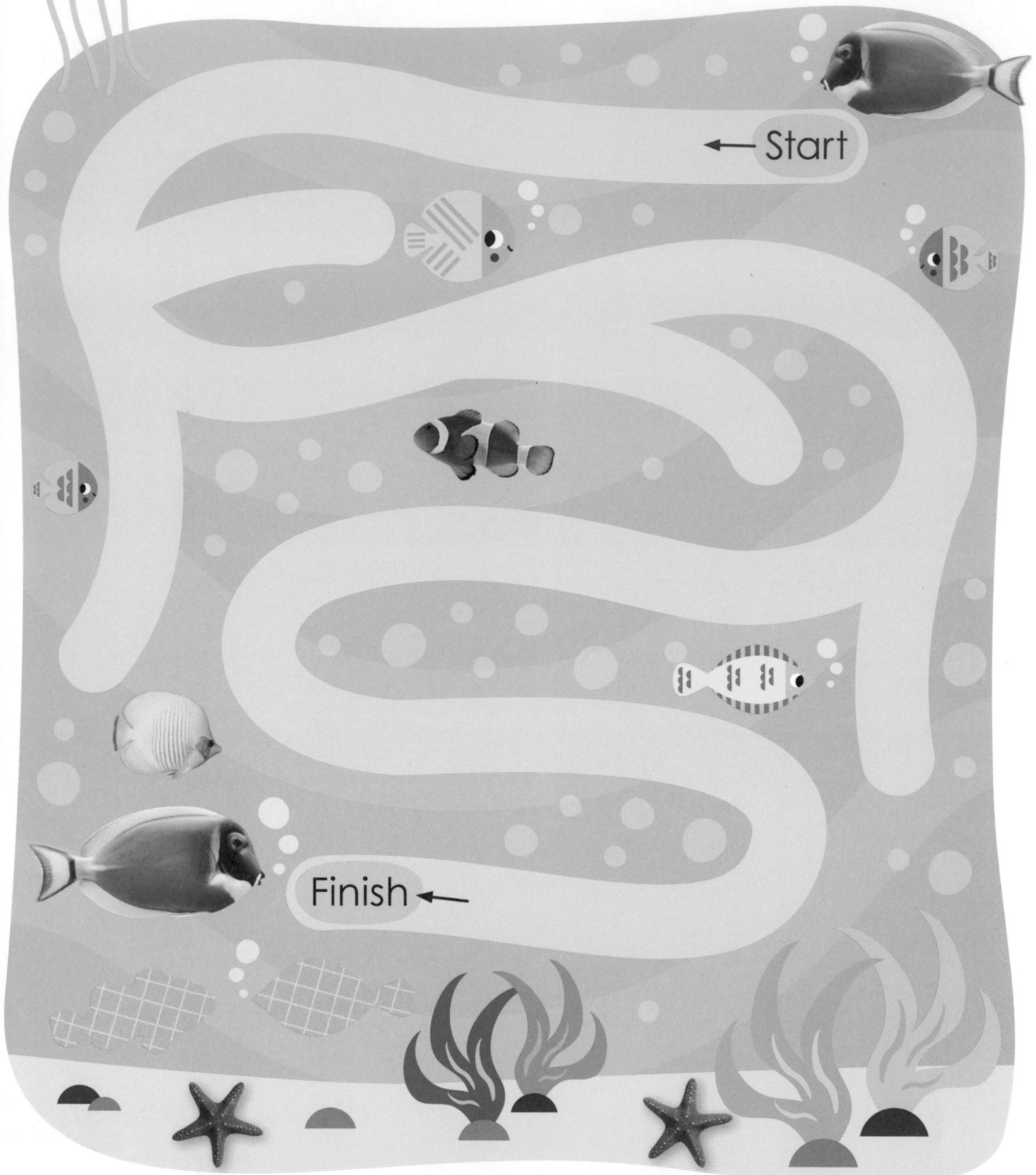

Start

Finish

Playground games

Help the children find the playground.

Start→

→Finish

Home time

Help the family bike home.

Puppy love

Help the dog find its puppy.

Start →

Finish

z z Z

Story time

Help the teacher find the storybook.

Start →

→ Finish

Monster maze

Help the hero catch the monster.

Flower power

Help the bee fly around the flower.

Start

Finish

Playtime

Help the children find the toy box.

Start

Finish

Fly away home

Help the owl reach her owlets.

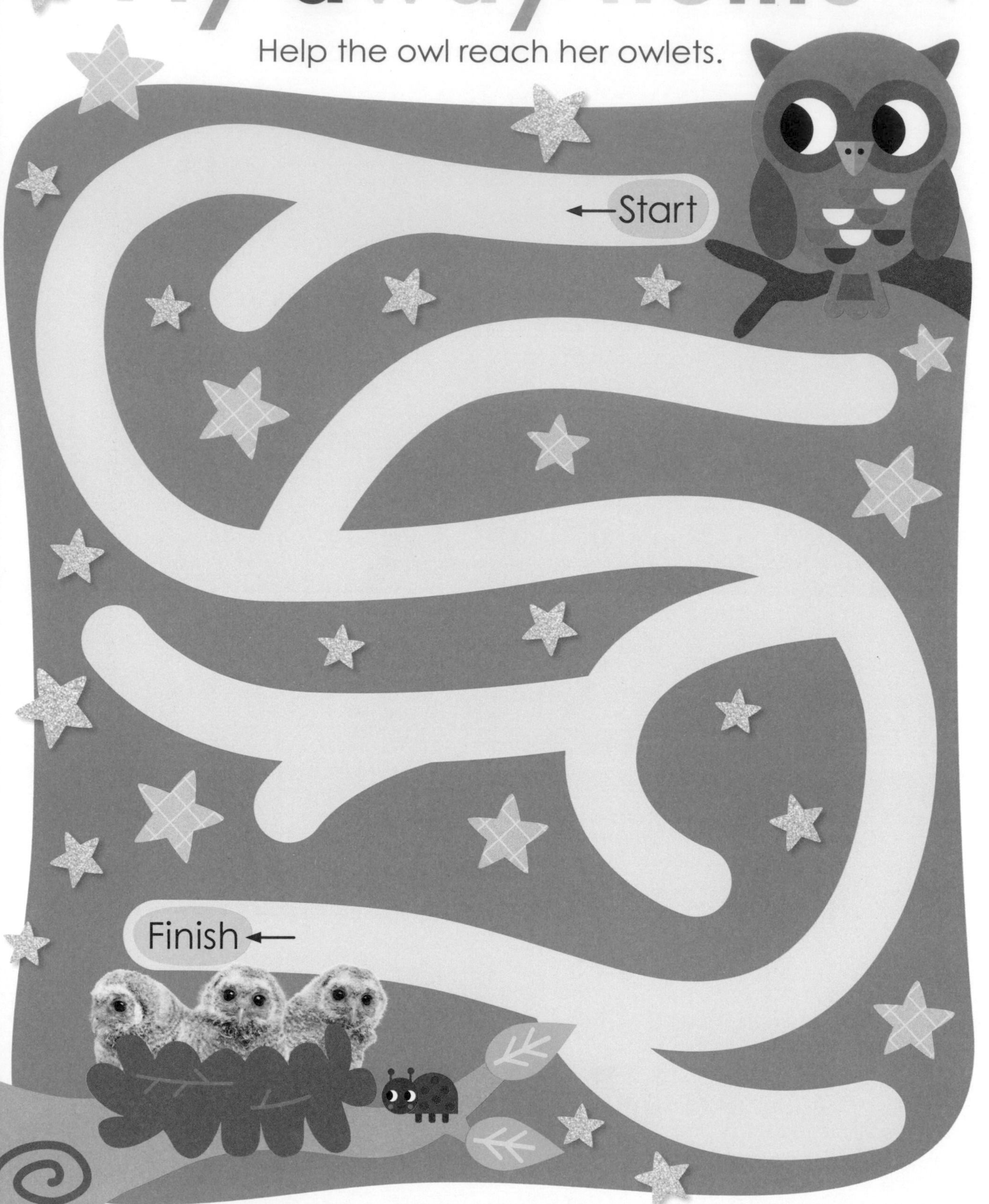

Tiger tangle

Find your way through the tiger's stripes.

Red

Trace these **red** things.

STOP

Color these things **red**.

Green

Trace these **green** things.

Color these things **green**.

Blue

Trace these **blue** things.

Color these things **blue**.

Trace these **orange** things.

Color these things **orange**.

Yellow

Trace these yellow things.

Color these things yellow.

Purple

Trace these **purple** things.

Color these things **purple**.

Pink

Trace these **pink** things.

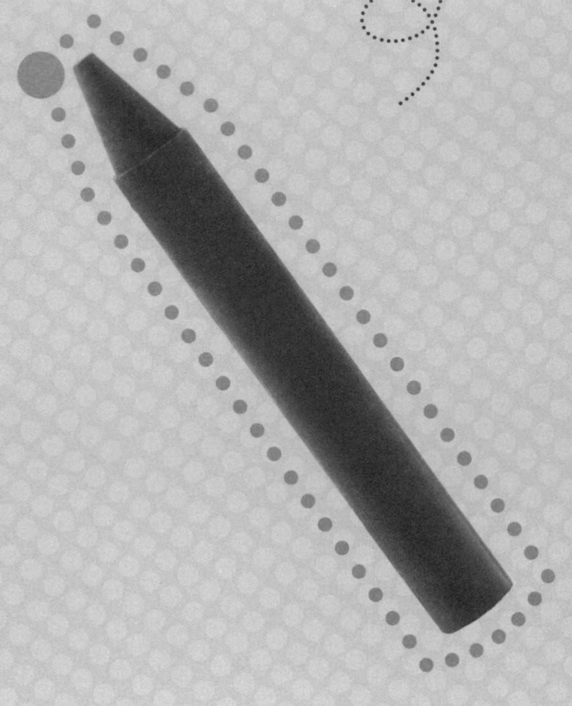

Color these things **pink**.

Brown

Trace these **brown** things.

Color these things **brown**.

Black

Trace these **black** things.

Color these things **black.**

White

Trace these white things.

Trace these white things.

Squares

Trace the **squares**.

Color Lily's square **blue**.

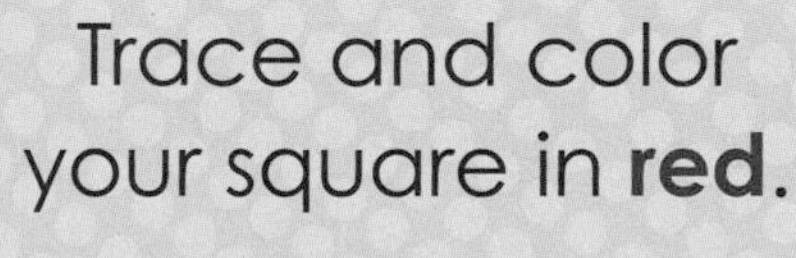

Trace and color your square in **red**.

Rectangles

Trace the **rectangles**.

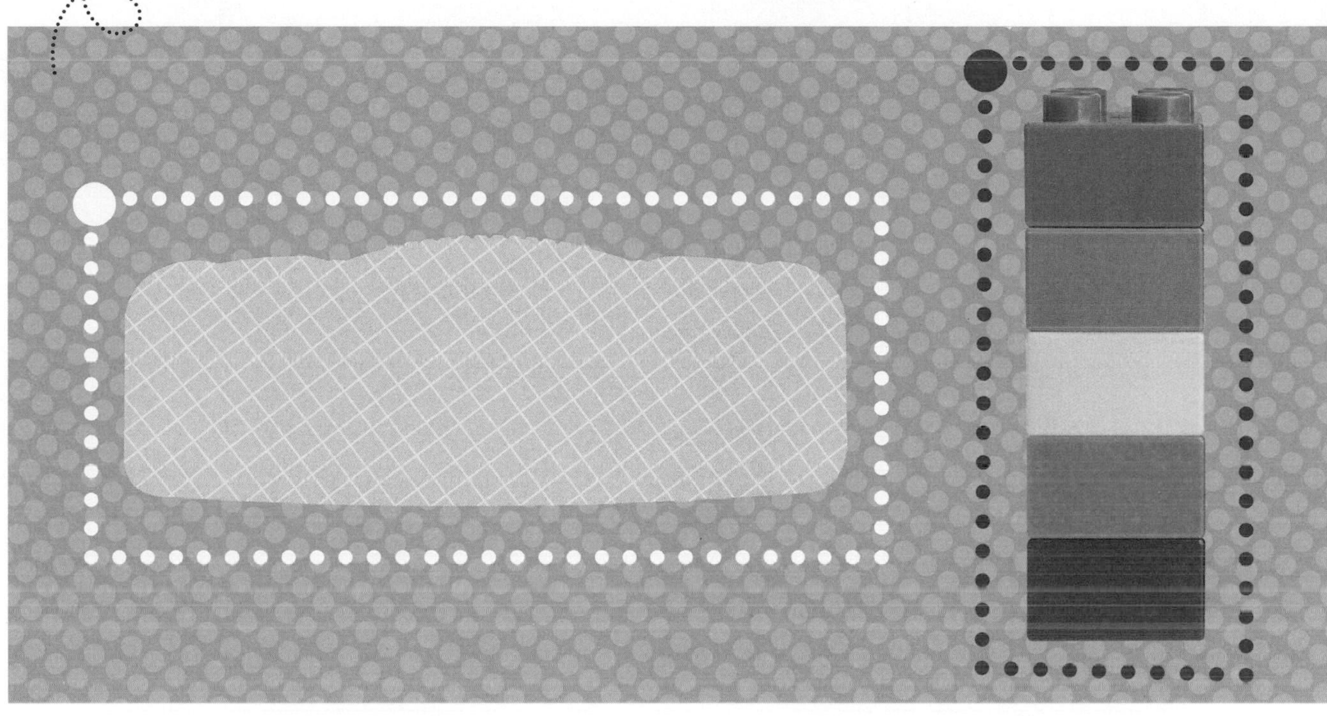

Color Jack's rectangle **green**.

Trace and color your rectangle in **yellow**.

Triangles

Trace the **triangles**.

Color Noah's triangle **orange**.

Trace and color your triangle in **purple**.

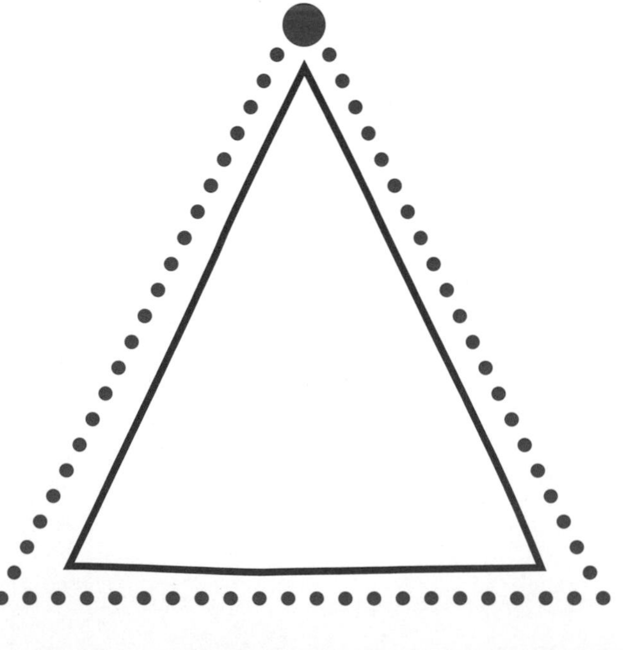

Circles

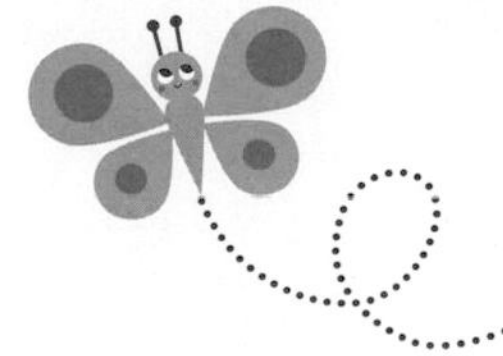

Trace the **circles**.

Color Ava's circle **pink**.

Trace and color your circle in **brown**.

Ovals

Trace the **ovals**.

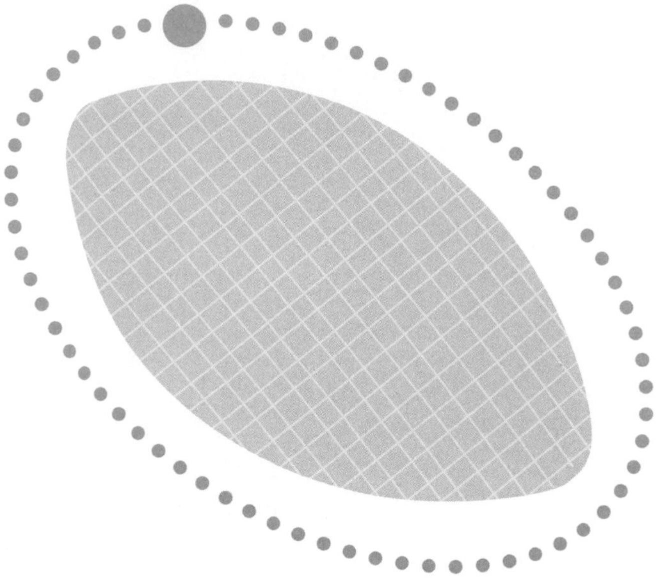

Color Abby's oval **orange**.

Trace and color your oval in **blue**.

Stars

Trace the **stars**.

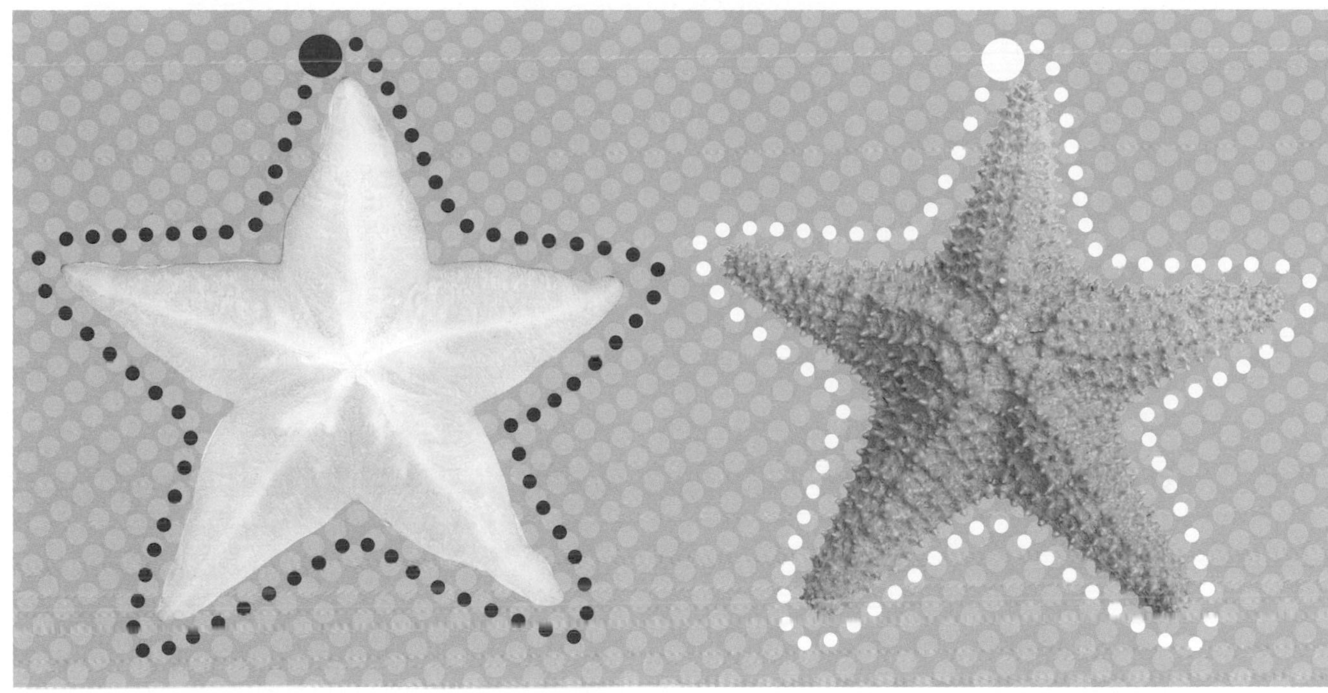

Color Ben's star yellow.

Trace and color your star in **green**.

Hearts

Trace the **hearts**.

Color Luke's heart **pink**.

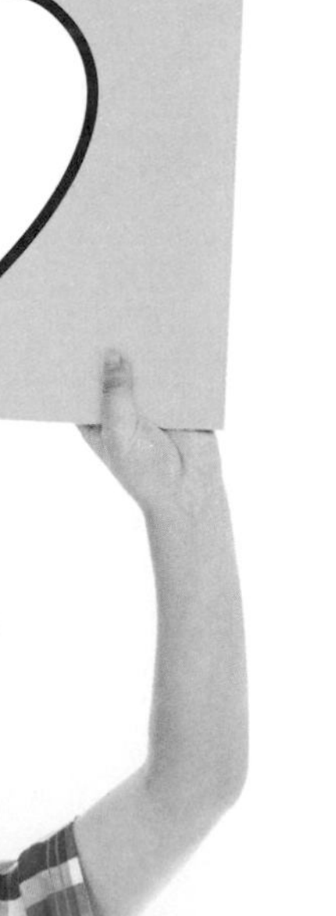

Trace and color your heart in **red**.

Arrows

Trace the **arrows.**

Color Olivia's arrow **green**.

Trace and color your arrow in **pink**.

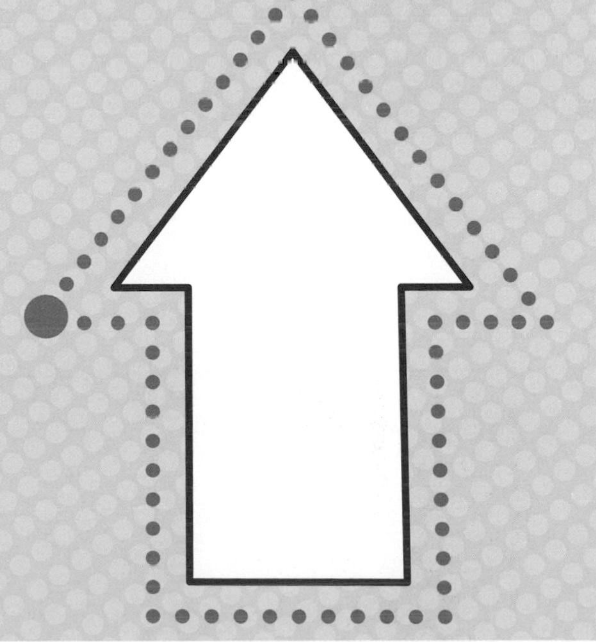

Match the shapes

Draw lines to match the shapes that are the same.

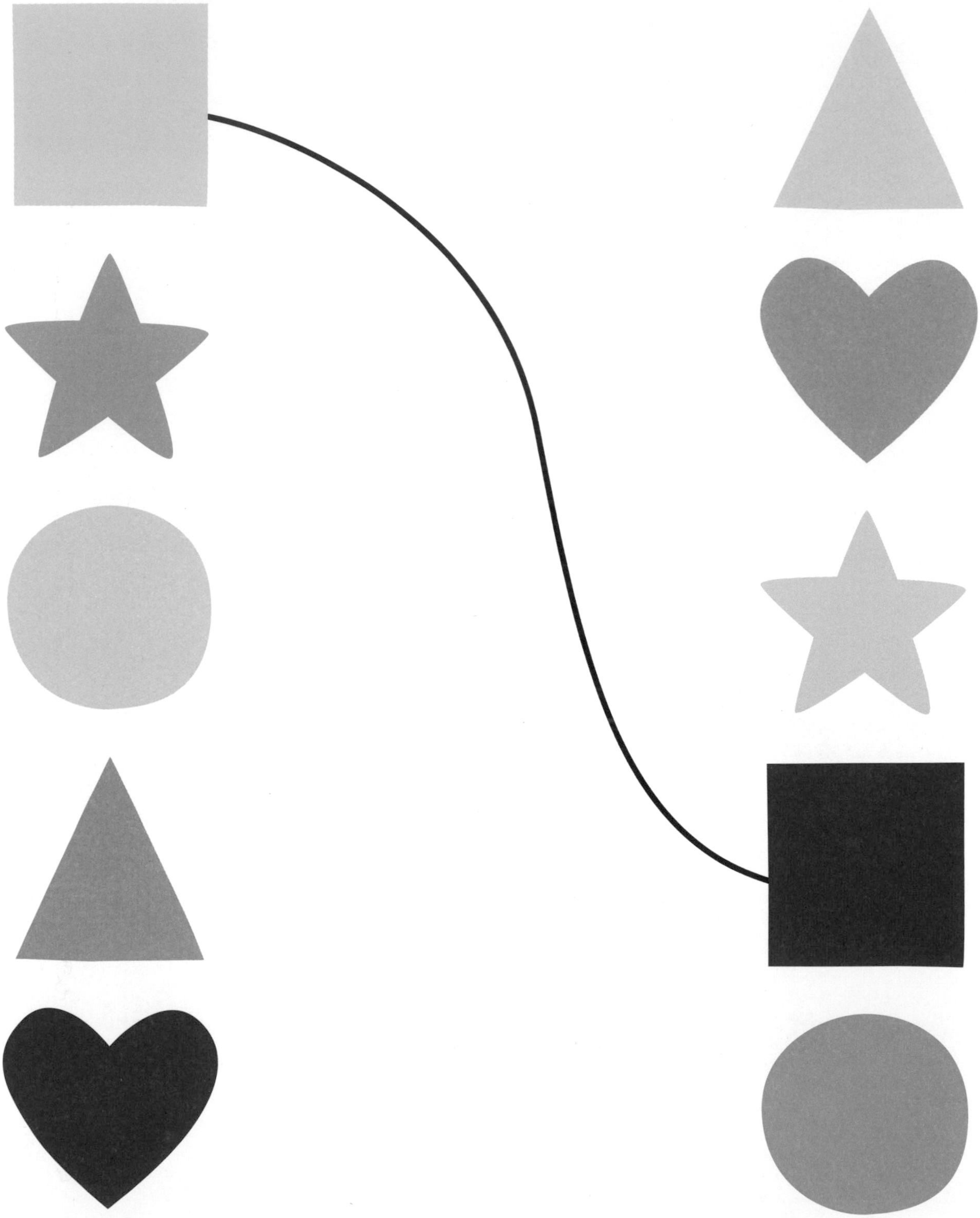

Match the objects

Draw lines to match the things that are the same shape.

Color the **A**.

Trace the letters with your finger.

Trace the dotted letters with your pencil.

Trace the uppercase and lowercase **a**'s.

Andy apple

Color the **B**.

Trace the letters with your finger.

Bb

banana

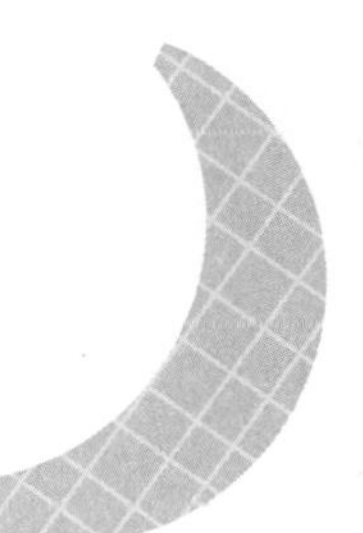

Trace the dotted letters with your pencil.

B B B b b b

Trace the uppercase and lowercase **b**'s.

Belle boat

Color the **C**.

Trace the letters with your finger.

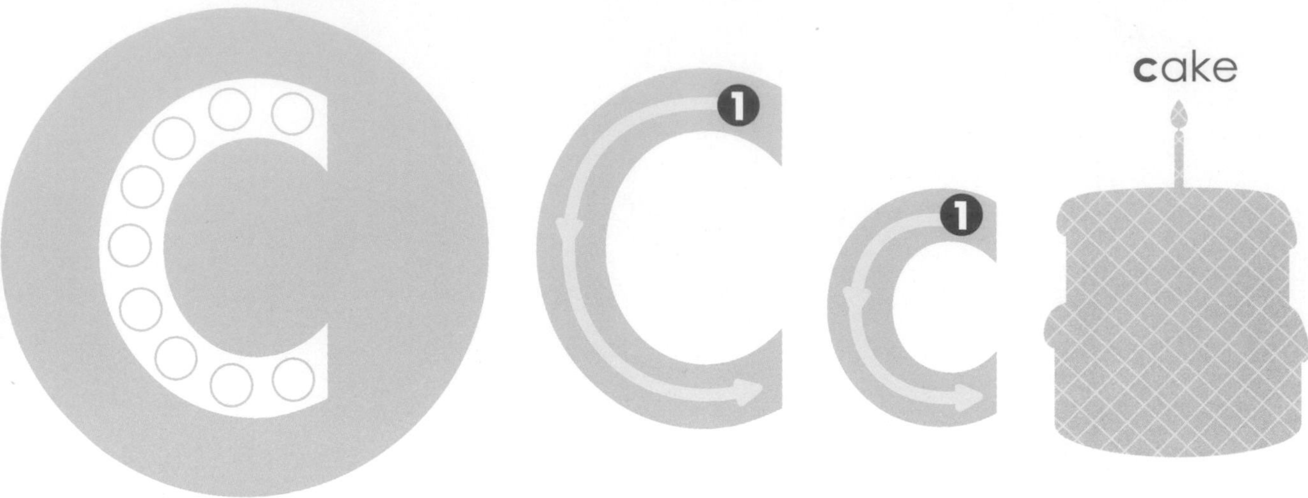

Trace the dotted letters with your pencil.

Trace the uppercase and lowercase **c**'s.

Clara

cat

Color the **D**.

Trace the letters with your finger.

Trace the dotted letters with your pencil.

Trace the uppercase and lowercase **d**'s.

Dylan doll

Color the **E**.

Trace the letters with your finger.

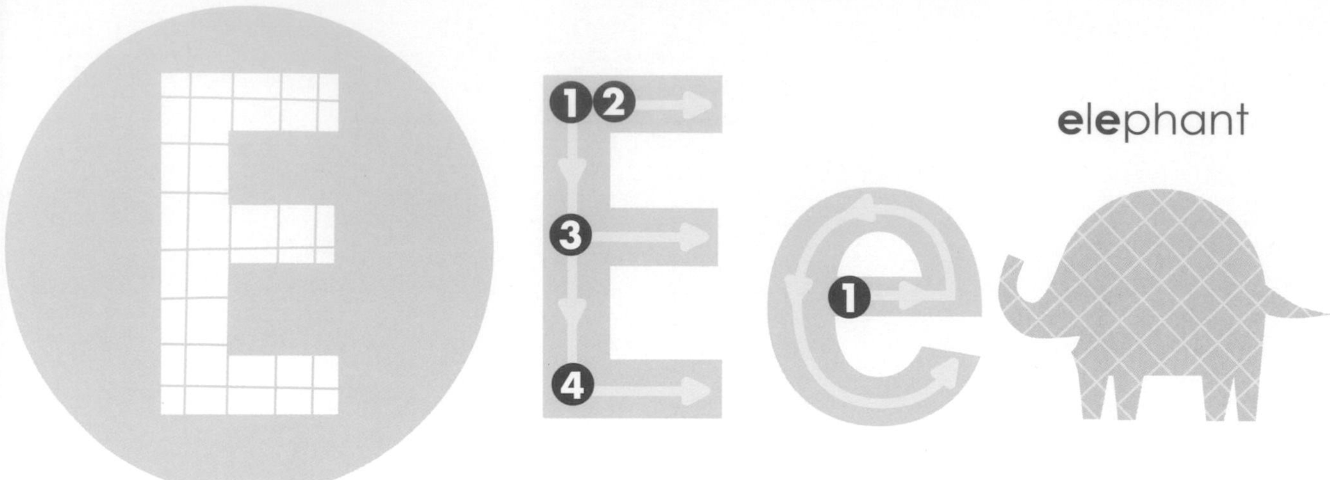

Trace the dotted letters with your pencil.

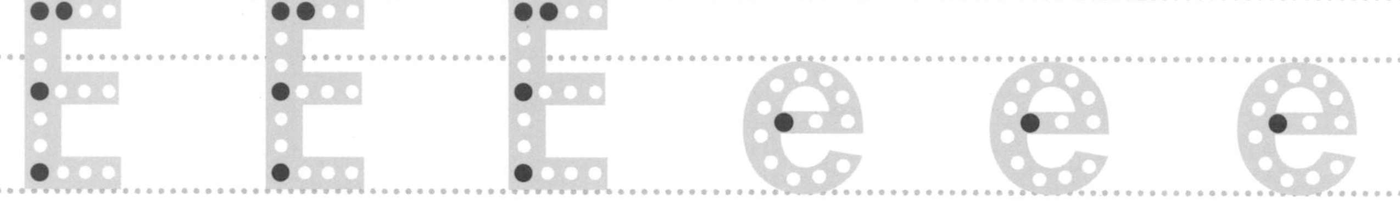

Trace the uppercase and lowercase **e**'s.

Color the **F**.

Trace the letters with your finger.

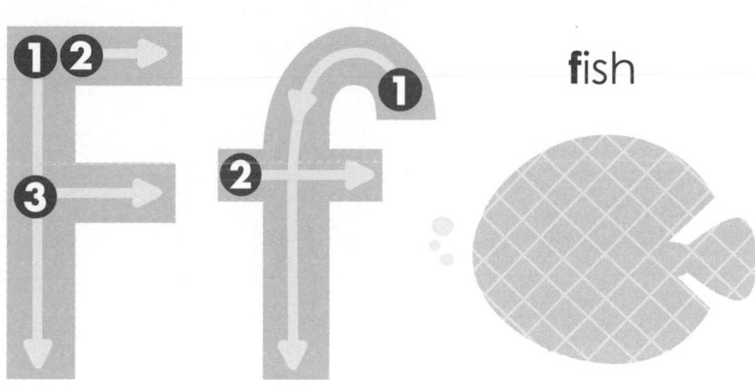

Trace the dotted letters with your pencil.

Trace the uppercase and lowercase **f**'s.

Color the **G**.

Trace the letters with your finger.

Trace the dotted letters with your pencil.

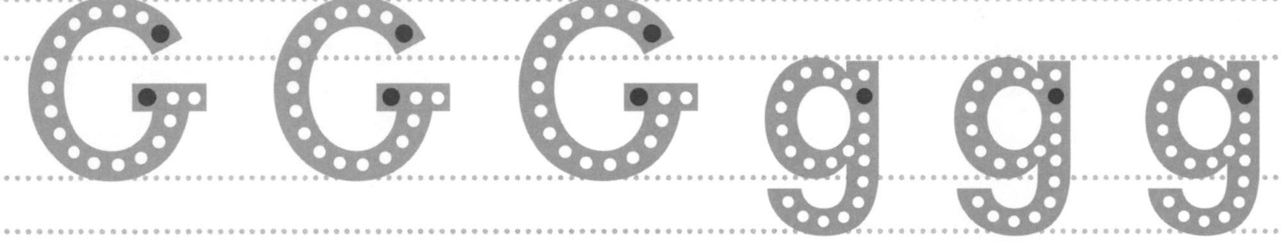

Trace the uppercase and lowercase **g**'s.

Grace goat

Color the **H**.

Trace the letters with your finger.

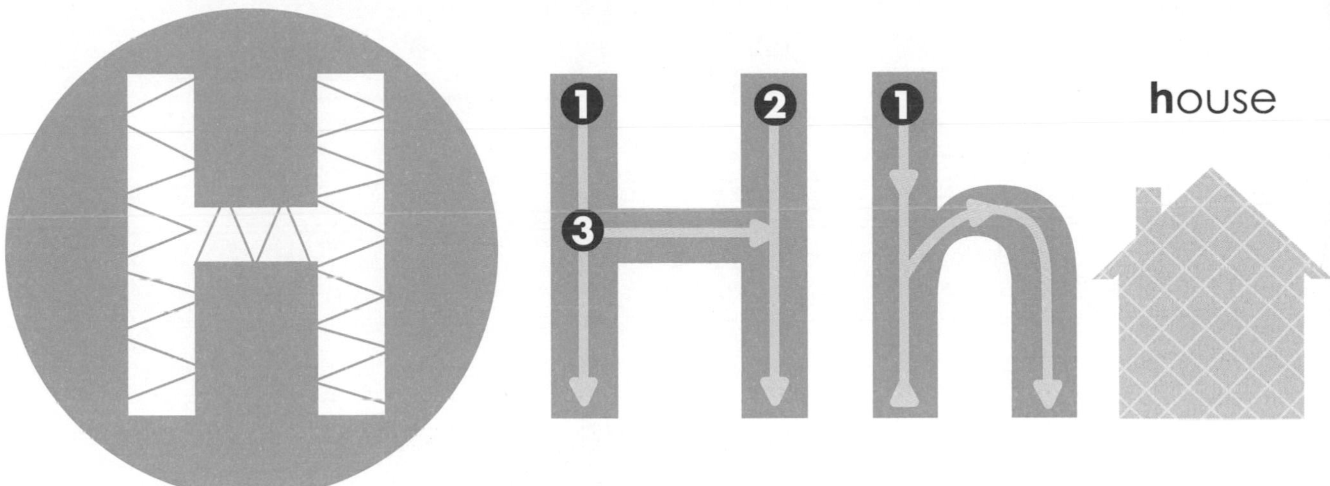

Trace the dotted letters with your pencil.

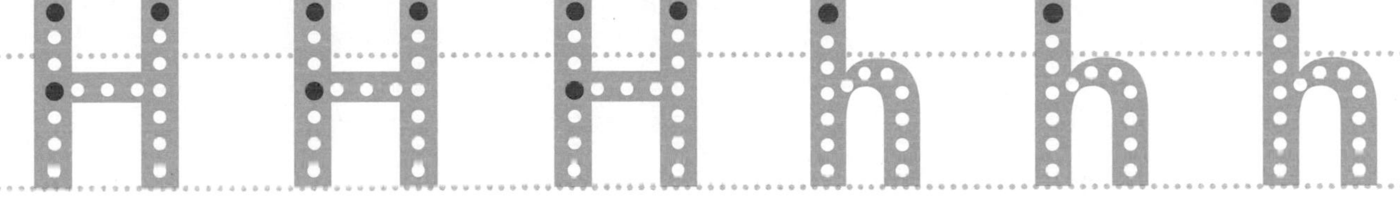

Trace the uppercase and lowercase **h**'s.

Henry horse

Color the **I**.

Trace the letters with your finger.

Trace the dotted letters.

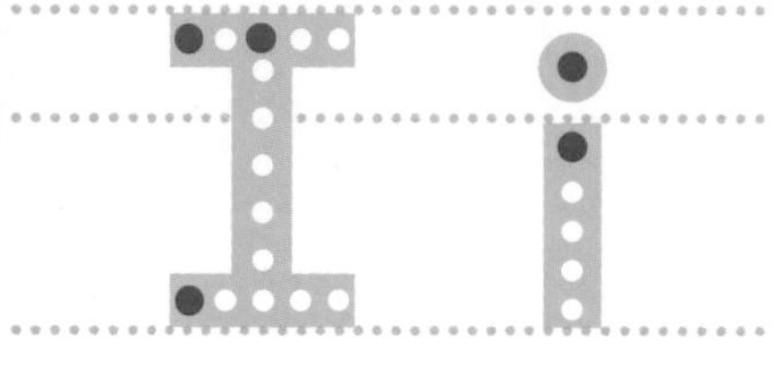

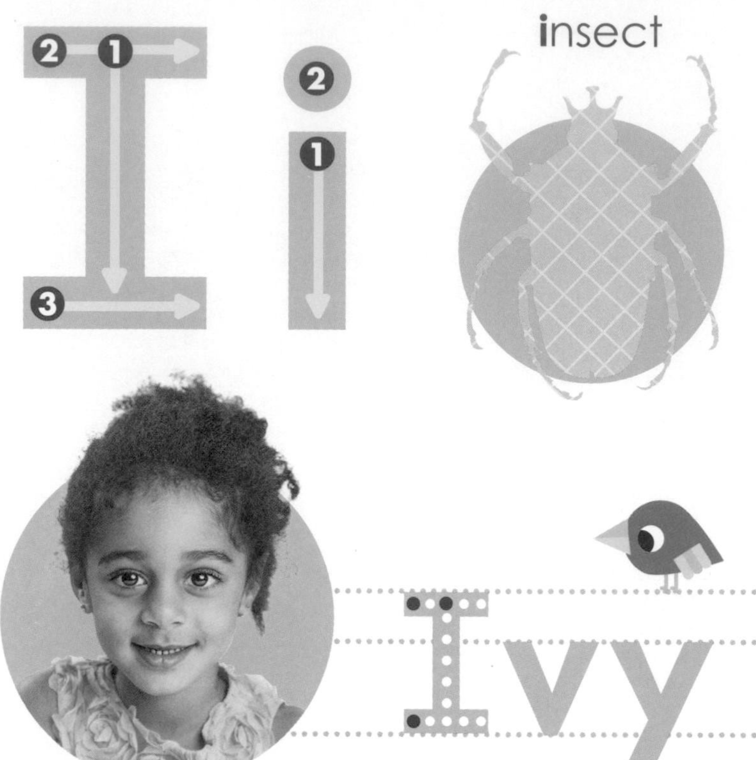

Color the **J**.

Trace the letters with your finger.

Trace the dotted letters.

Color the **K**. Trace the letters with your finger.

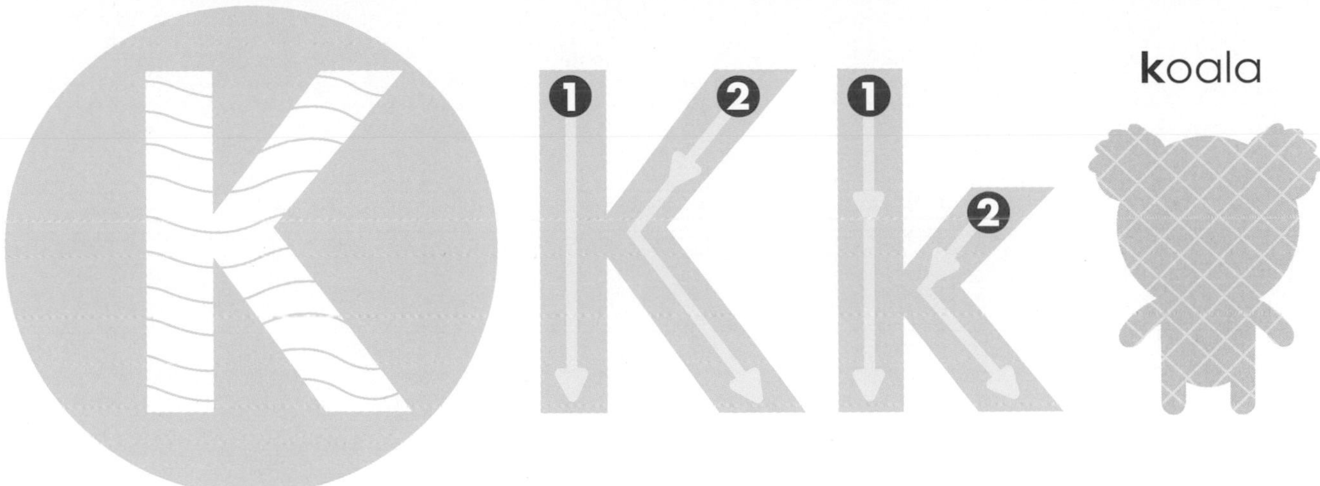

Trace the dotted letters with your pencil.

Trace the uppercase and lowercase **k**'s.

Color the **L**.

Trace the letters with your finger.

lamp

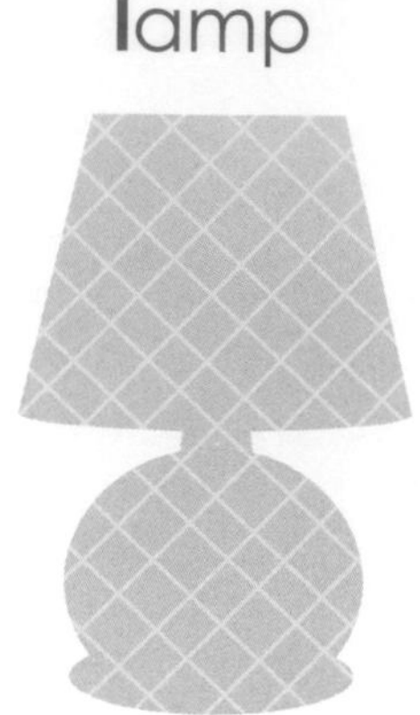

Trace the dotted letters with your pencil.

Trace the uppercase and lowercase **l**'s.

Luke lemon

Color the **M**.

Trace the letters with your finger.

Trace the dotted letters.

Color the **N**.

Trace the letters with your finger.

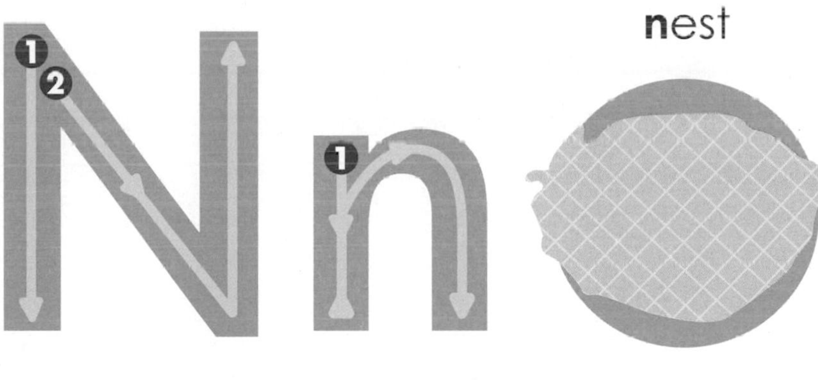

Trace the dotted letters.

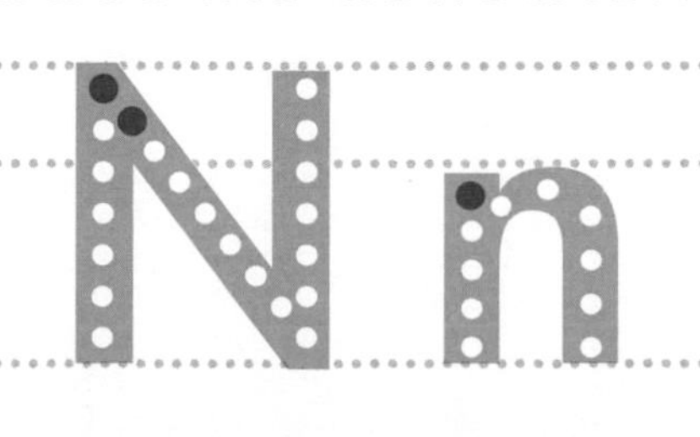

Color the **O**.

Trace the letters with your finger.

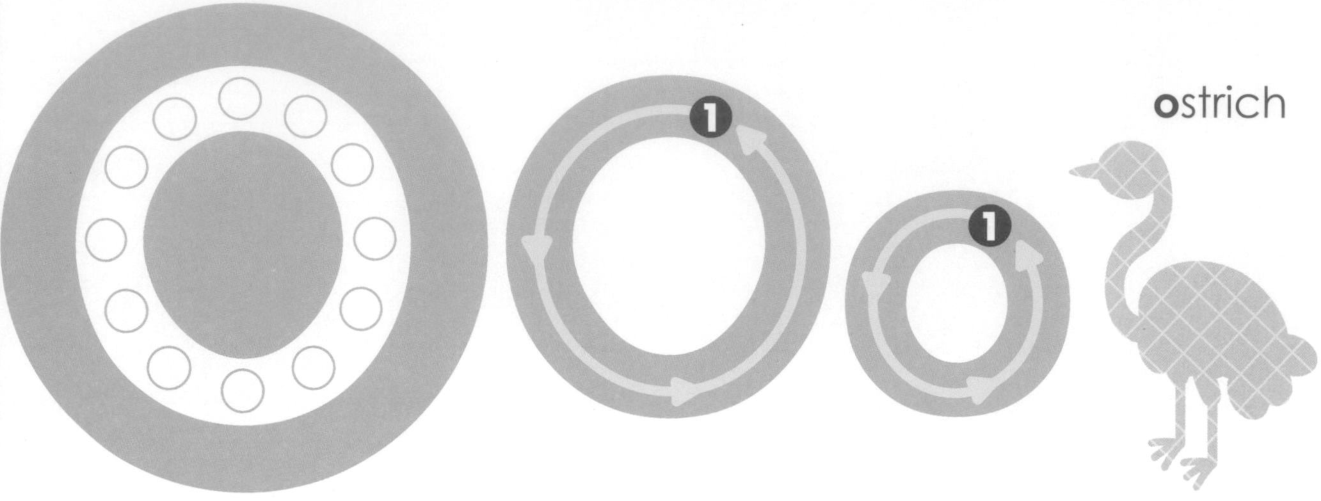

Trace the dotted letters with your pencil.

Trace the uppercase and lowercase **o**'s.

Color the **P**.

Trace the letters with your finger.

Trace the dotted letters with your pencil.

Trace the uppercase and lowercase **p**'s.

Piper panda

Color the **Q**.

Trace the letters with your finger.

Trace the dotted letters.

Color the **R**.

Trace the letters with your finger.

Trace the dotted letters.

Color the **S**.

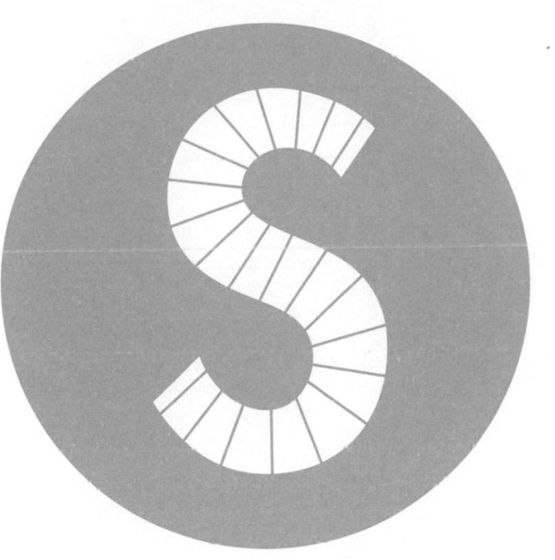

Trace the letters with your finger.

snake

Trace the dotted letters with your pencil.

Trace the uppercase and lowercase **s**'s.

Color the **T**.

Trace the letters with your finger.

Trace the dotted letters with your pencil.

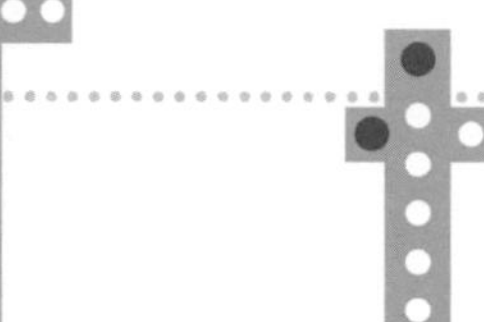

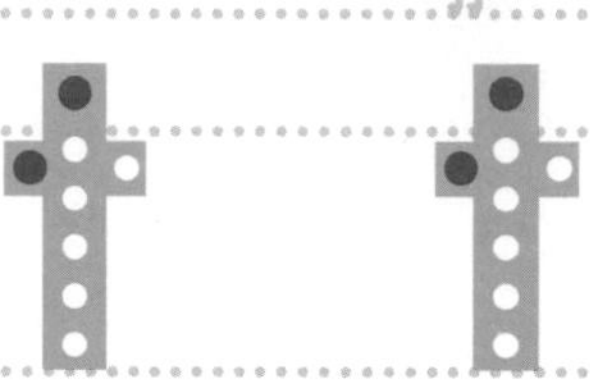

Trace the uppercase and lowercase **t**'s.

Tim tiger

Color the **U**.

Trace the letters with your finger.

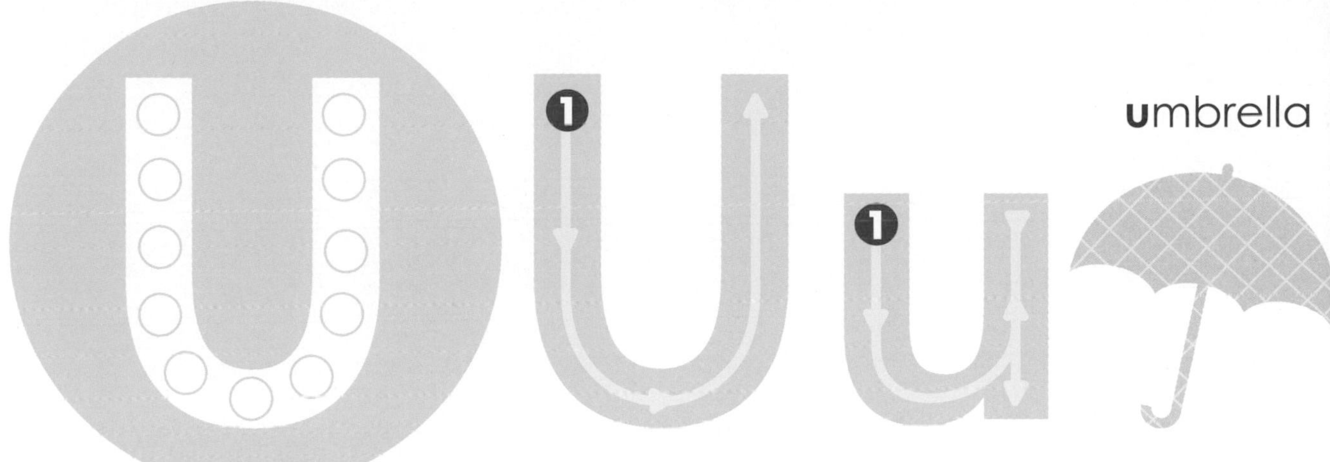

Trace the dotted letters with your pencil.

Trace the uppercase and lowercase **u**'s.

Una

up

ABC

Color the **V**.

Trace the letters with your finger.

V v

vet

Trace the dotted letters.

V v

Vicky

Color the **W**.

Trace the letters with your finger.

W w

wasp

Trace the dotted letters.

W w

Will

Color the **X**.

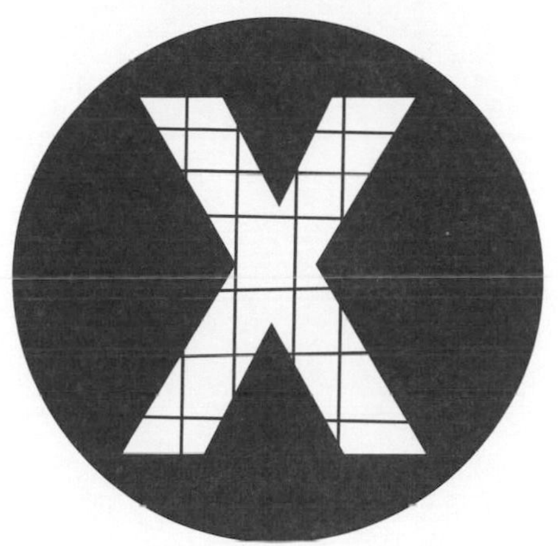

Trace the letters with your finger.

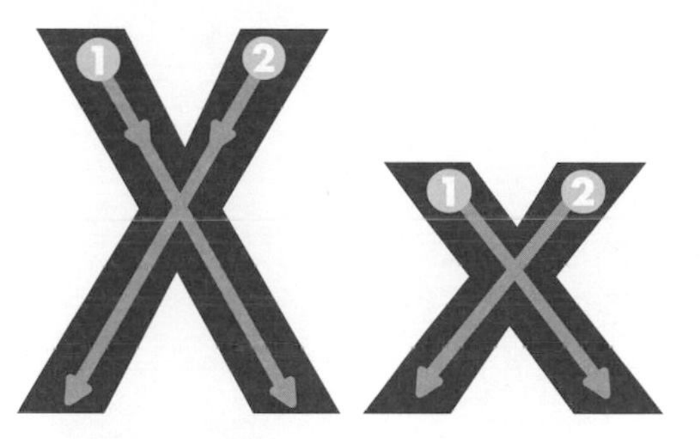

X-ray

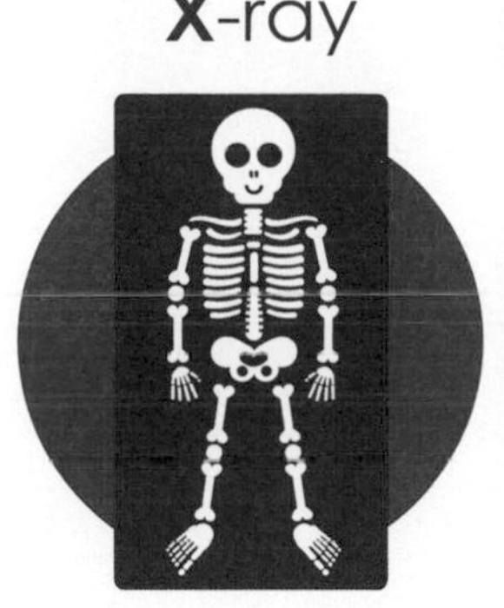

Trace the dotted letters.

Color the **Y**.

Trace the letters with your finger.

yo-**y**o

Trace the dotted letters.

Y y

Yosef

Color the **Z**.

Trace the letters with your finger.

Z z

zebra

Trace the dotted letters.

Z Z Z z z z

Trace the uppercase and lowercase **z**'s.

Zara

zero

Read the uppercase and lowercase alphabet.
Then trace the letters.

Aa Bb Cc Dd

Ee Ff Gg Hh

Ii Jj Kk Ll Mm

Nn Oo Pp Qq

Rr Ss Tt Uu Vv

Ww Xx Yy Zz

Snake starts with s

Say the words. What sound do they start with?

snake ski sing

Circle the words that start with the **s** sound.

swan

sign

bus

Teddy starts with t

Say the words. What sound do they start with?

turkey

top

teddy

Draw lines from the **t** to the words that start with **t**.

tiger

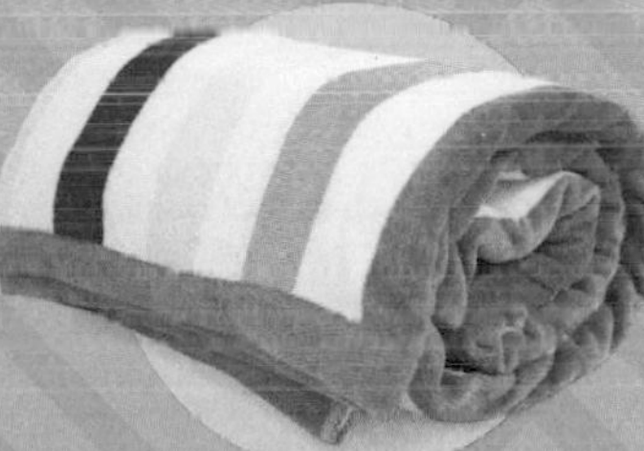

towel

t

ball

table

Panda starts with p

Say the words. What sound do they start with?

panda pie pirate

Say the words aloud and circle the **p**'s.

puppet

puppy

Nest starts with n

Say the words. What sound do they start with?

nest nurse nine

Check the words that begin with **n**.

nuts

nose

socks

net

Mouse starts with m

Say the words. What sound do they start with?

mouse map mittens

Circle the words that start with the **m** sound.

mug

hat

monkey

Doll starts with d

Say the words. What sound do they start with?

doll duck dog

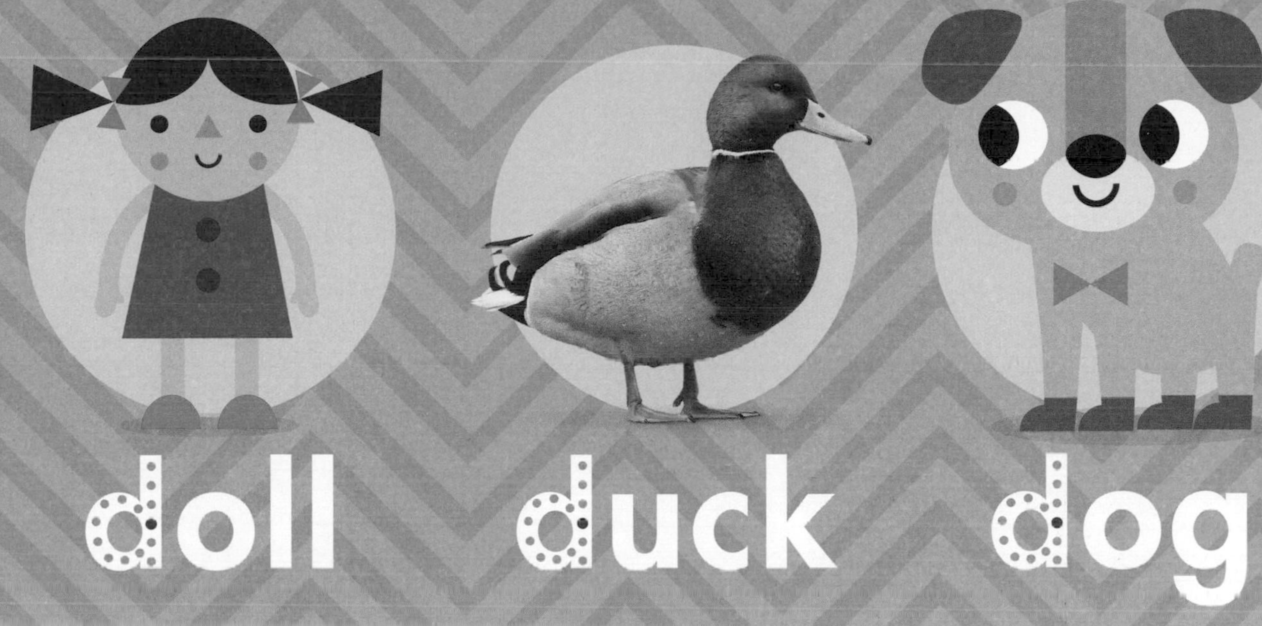

Draw lines from the **d** to the words that start with **d**.

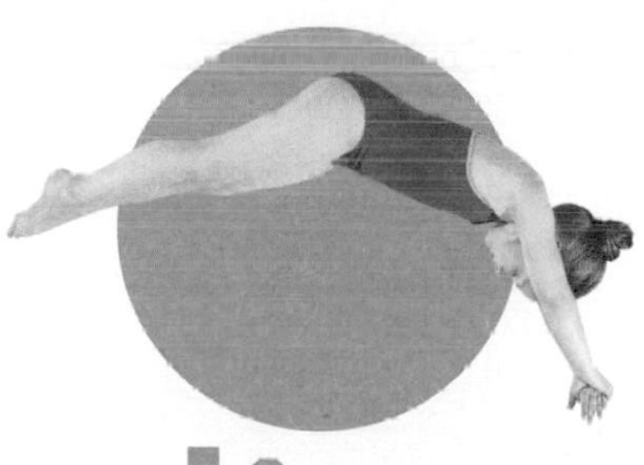

dive

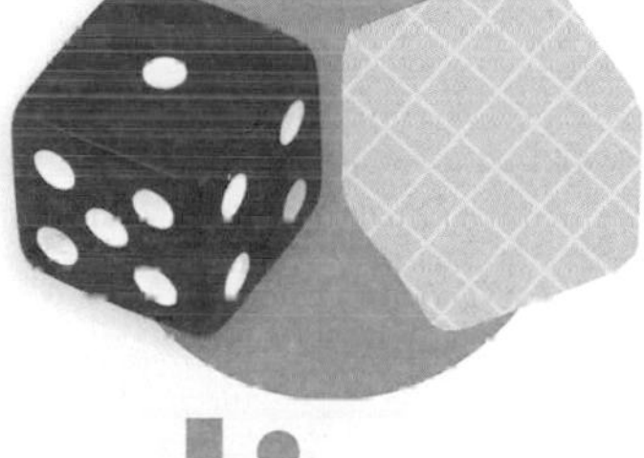

dice

d

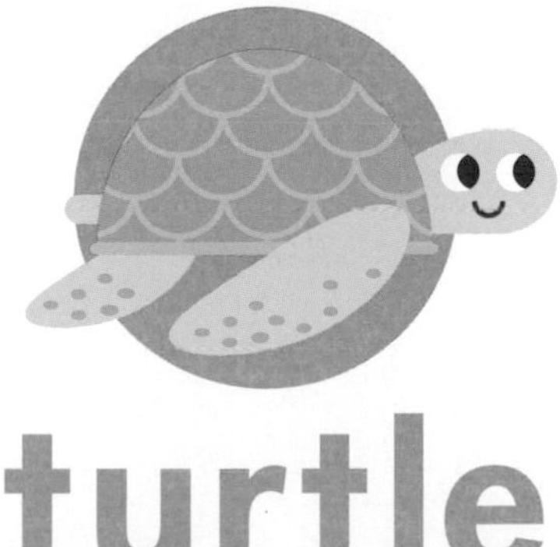

turtle

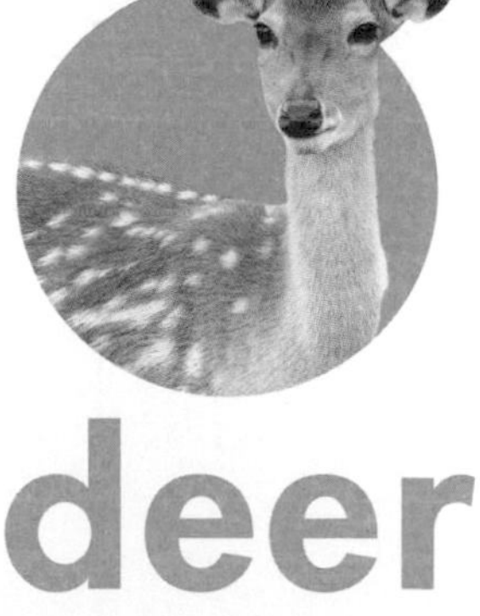

deer

Goat starts with g

Say the words. What sound do they start with?

goat grapes gift

Say the words aloud and circle the **g**'s.

goggles giggle

Robot starts with r

Say the words. What sound do they start with?

Check the words that begin with **r**.

rhino ☐

radio ☐

rope ☐

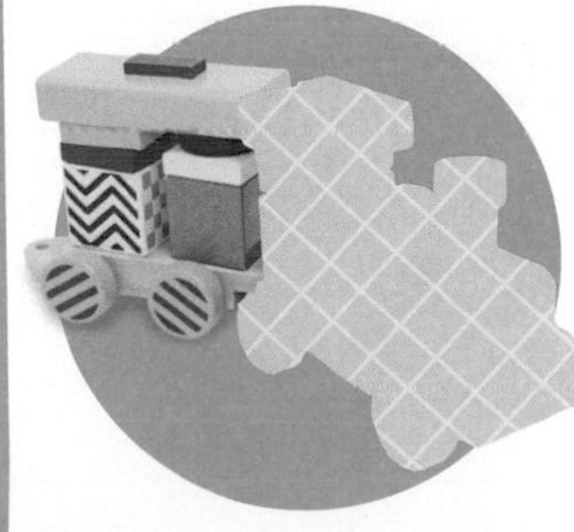

train ☐

Car starts with c

Say the words. What sound do they start with?

car coat carrot

Circle the words that start with the **c** sound.

cow

fish

comb

Kitten starts with k

Say the words. What sound do they start with?

kitten key king

Draw lines from the **k** to the words that start with **k**.

tent

kiss

koala

kite

Bus starts with b

Say the words. What sound do they start with?

bus bird bee

Say the words aloud and circle the **b**'s.

bib bubble

Hippo starts with h

Say the words. What sound do they start with?

hippo hen honey

Check the words that begin with **h**.

house ☐

frog ☐

hat ☐

horse ☐

Fish starts with f

Say the words. What sound do they start with?

fish fork fox

Circle the words that start with the **f** sound.

fairy

tree

feather

Jump starts with j

Say the words. What sound do they start with?

jump jar jigsaw

Draw lines from the **j** to the words that start with **j**.

jacket

j

jewels

juice

insect

Leaf starts with l

Say the words. What sound do they start with?

leaf **lamb** **lime**

Say the words aloud and circle the **l**'s.

lily **lollipop**

Vet starts with v

Say the words. What sound do they start with?

vet vest vase

Check the words that begin with **v.**

crab ☐

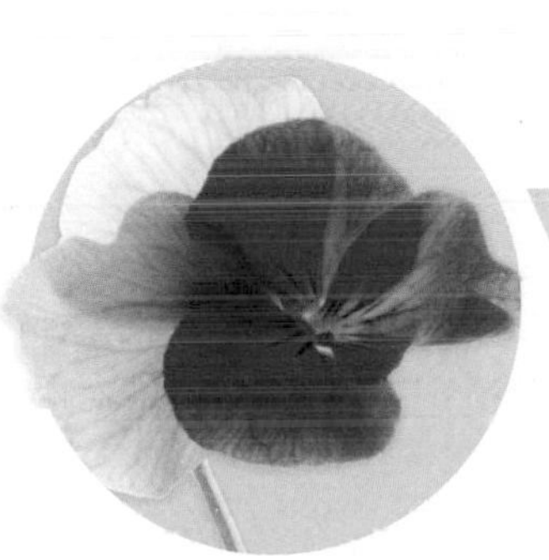

violet ☐

violin ☐

van ☐

Watch starts with w

Say the words. What sound do they start with?

watch web wagon

Circle the words that start with the **w** sound.

snail

worm

wig

Yo-yo starts with y

Say the words. What sound do they start with?

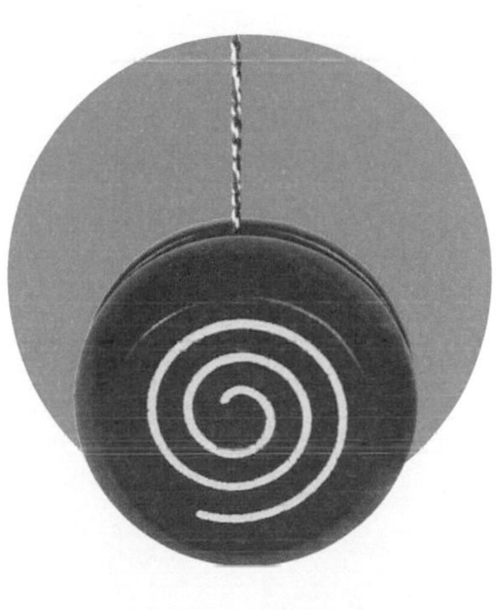

yo-yo yak yawn

Draw lines from the **y** to the words that start with **y**.

truck

yell

yellow

yogurt

Quiet starts with q

Say the words. What sound do they start with?

quiet queen quail

Circle the words that start with the **q** sound.

quack

bear

quilt

Fox ends with x

Say the words. What sound do they end with?

six

box

Check the words that have an **x** in them.

mix

taxi

sock

Zebra starts with z

Say the words. What sound do they start with?

zebra zero zoo

Say the words aloud and circle the **z**'s.

zigzag buzz

Match the sounds

Draw lines to match the words that start with the same sound.

sun pig

heart ball

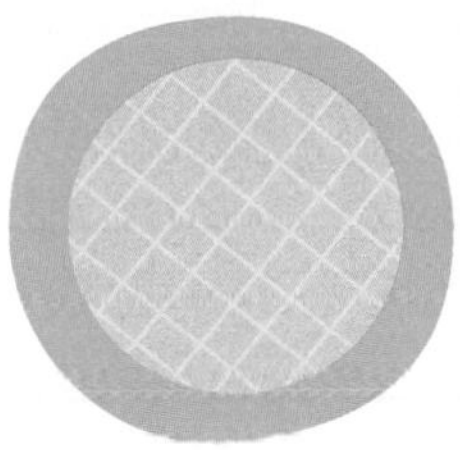

cat cup

beetle saw

pen hand

Match the rhymes

Say the words. Draw lines to match the rhymes.

cat

dog

frog

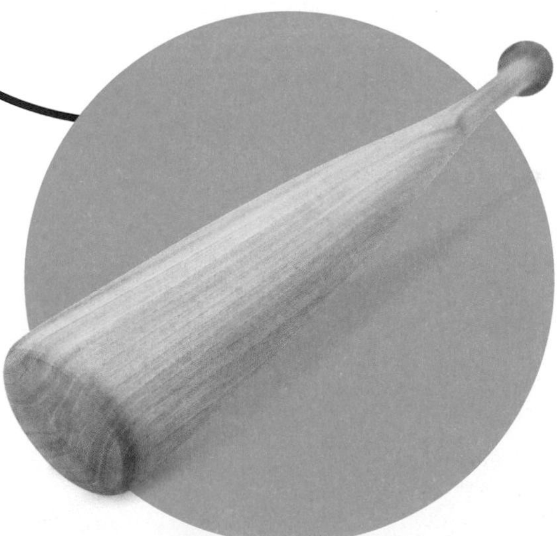

bat

Circle the rhyme

Circle the word that rhymes.

mouse

house

cup

car

snake star

Match the rhymes

Draw lines to match the rhymes.

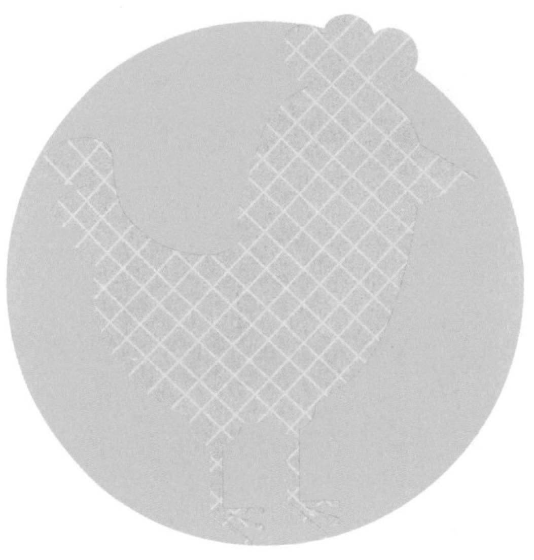

hen

dice

ice

pen

Circle the rhyme

Circle the word that rhymes.

sock

clock cake

duck

truck ball

Connect the rhymes

Draw lines from the **pug** to the things that rhyme with it.

Find the rhymes

Circle the words that rhyme with **wing**.

Connect the rhymes

Draw lines from the **skate** to the things that rhyme with it.

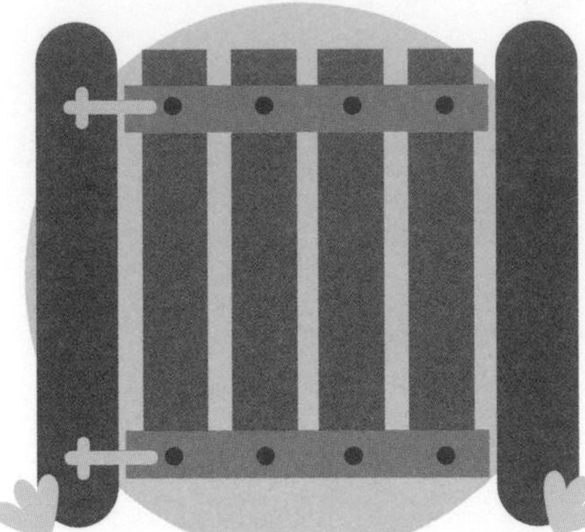

eight

gate

skate

cat

plate

Find the rhymes

Circle the words that rhyme with **nail**.

whale

teddy

plane

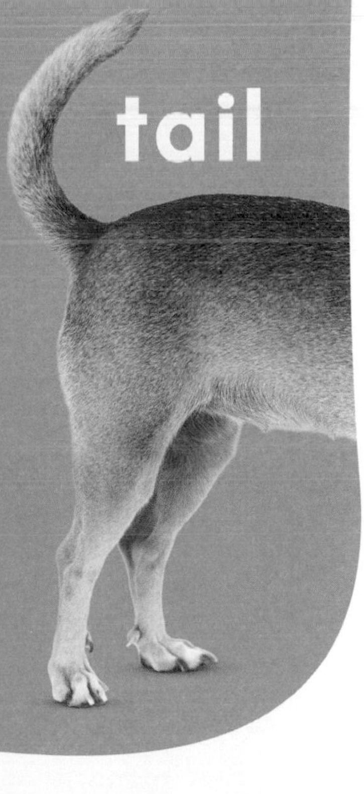

tail

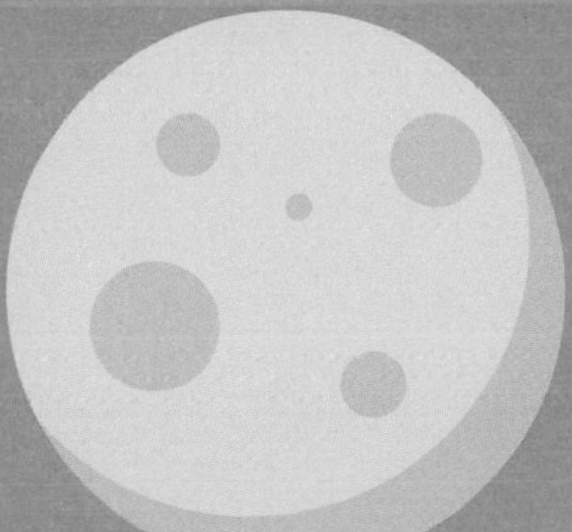

moon

snail

Match the rhymes

Draw lines to match the rhymes.

snake

cake

man

can

Circle the rhyme

Circle the word that rhymes.

chick

rocket brick

shark

park flower

What's wrong?

Circle the word that doesn't rhyme.

bun

baby

run

pot

hop

mop

Rhyming words

Trace the rhymes.

10

ten

pen

pig

dig

What's wrong?

Circle the word that doesn't rhyme.

cat cap clap

call ball bell

Rhyming words

Trace the rhymes.

Match the rhymes

Draw lines to match the rhymes.

jet

honey

vet

shark

money

bark

Rhyming words

Trace the rhymes.

Match the rhymes

Draw lines to match the rhymes.

Rhyming words

Trace the rhymes.

bear

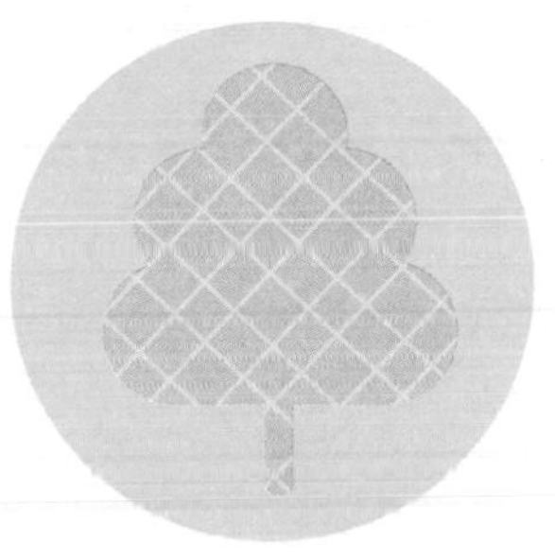

bone throne

Circle the rhyme

Circle the word that rhymes.

jeans

carrots beans

talk

walk dance

Rhyming words

Trace the rhymes.

snap cap

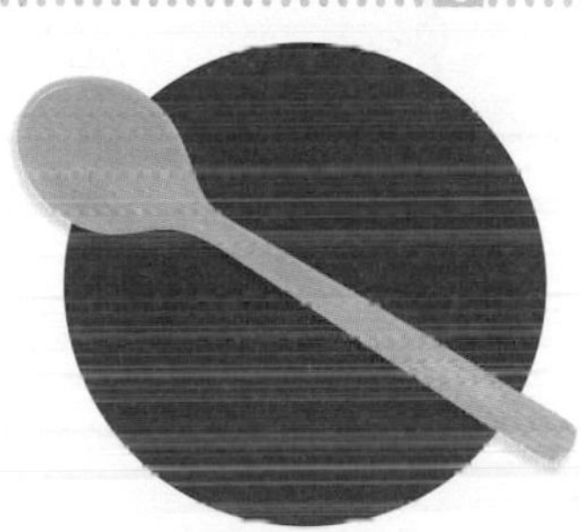

moon spoon

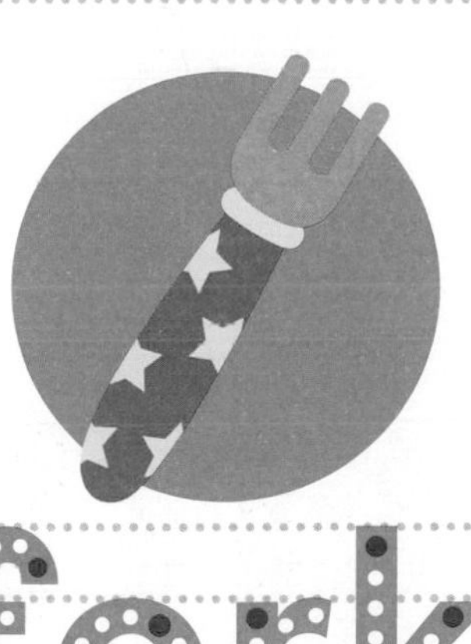

fork stork

Trace the letters with your finger.

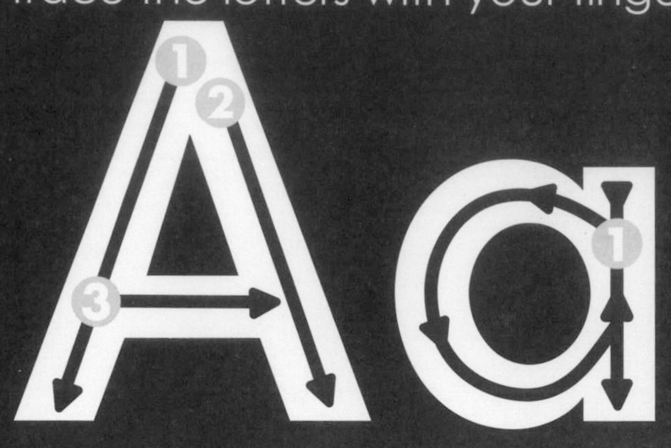

athlete

Trace the letters with your pencil.

Trace the letters with your finger.

bike

Trace the letters with your pencil.

bee

Trace the letters with your finger.

car

Trace the letters with your pencil.

cake

Trace the letters with your finger.

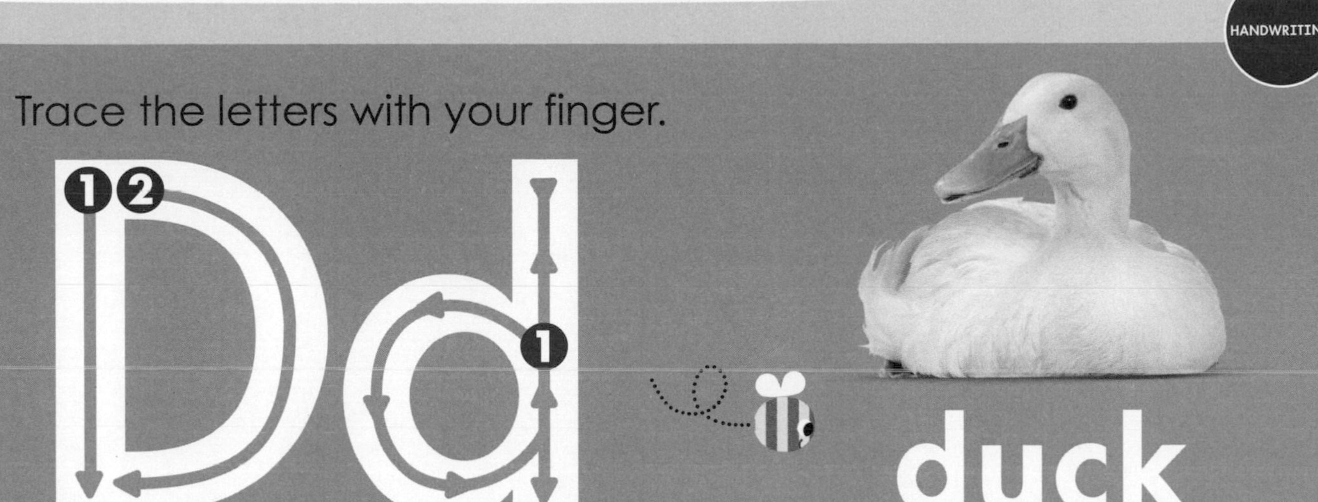

Trace the letters with your pencil.

Trace the letters with your finger.

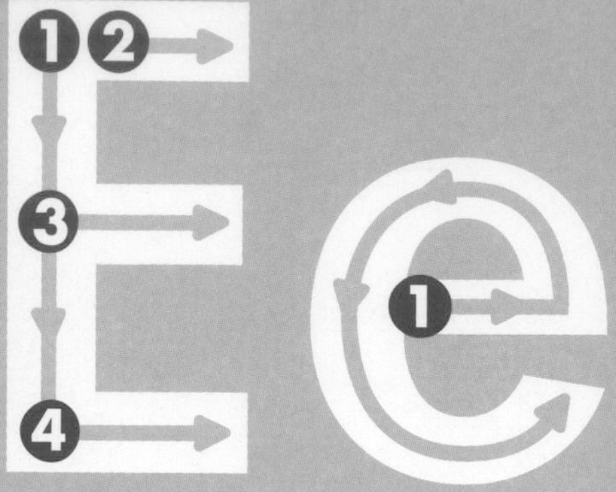

Trace the letters with your pencil.

Trace the letters with your finger.

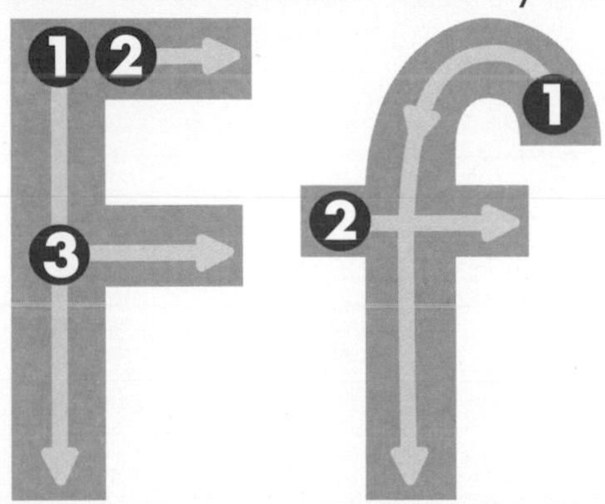

fairy

Trace the letters with your pencil.

F F F F F

Trace the letters with your finger.

gloves

Trace the letters with your pencil.

g g g g g

goat

Trace the letters with your finger.

Hh

house

Trace the letters with your pencil.

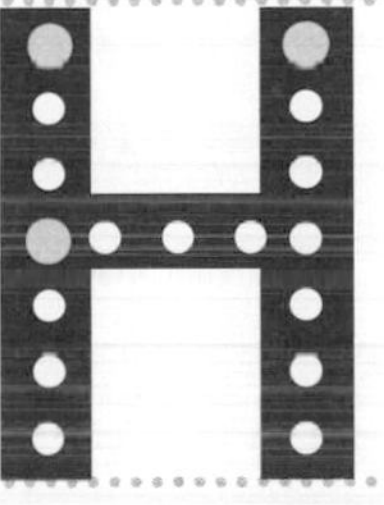

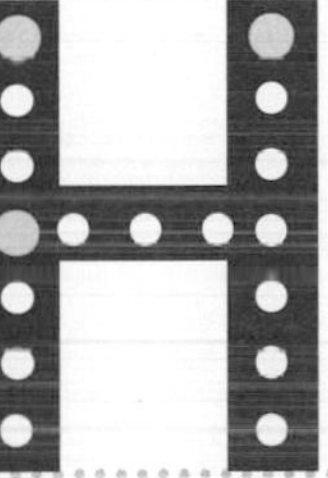

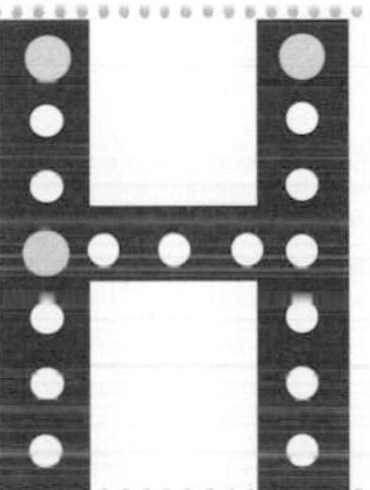

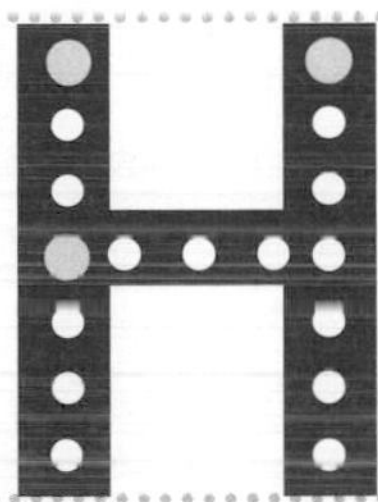

h h h h h

hen

Trace the letters with your finger and then with your pencil.

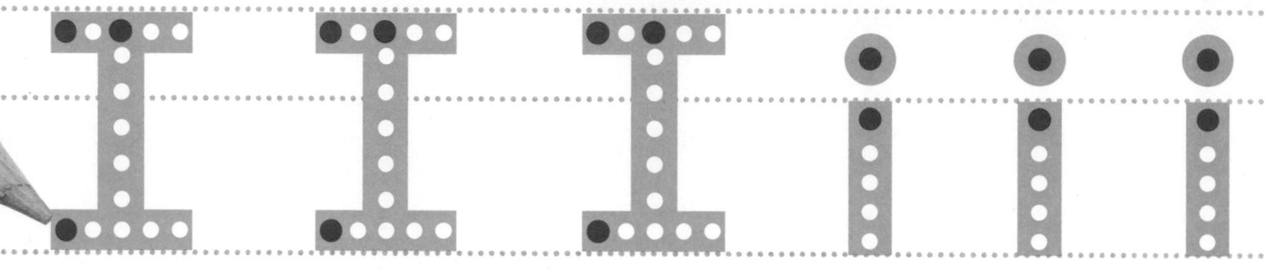

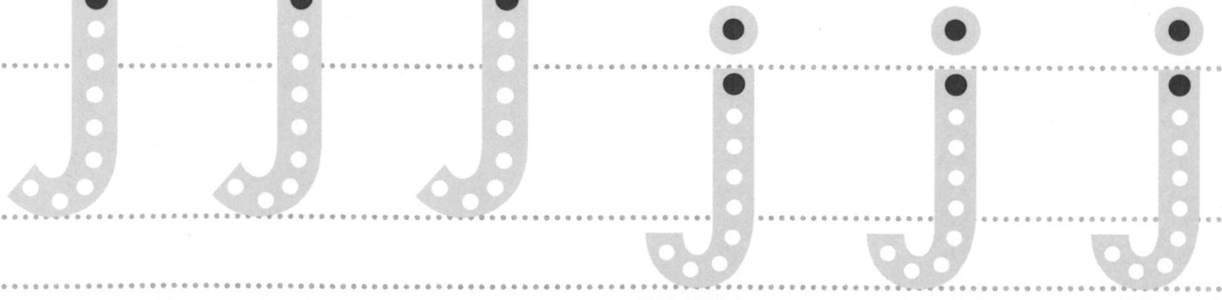

Trace the letters with your finger.

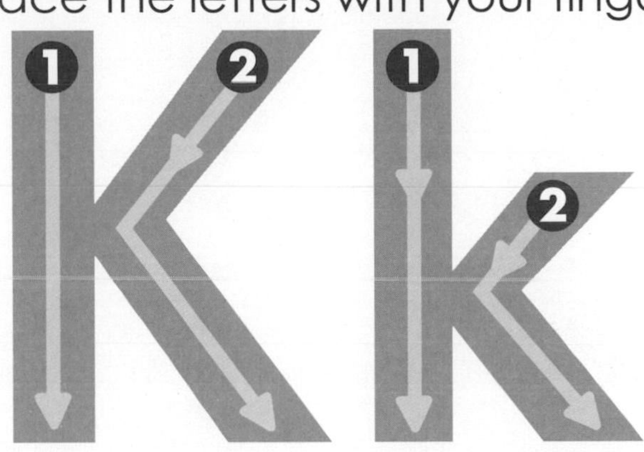

Trace the letters with your pencil.

Trace the letters with your finger.

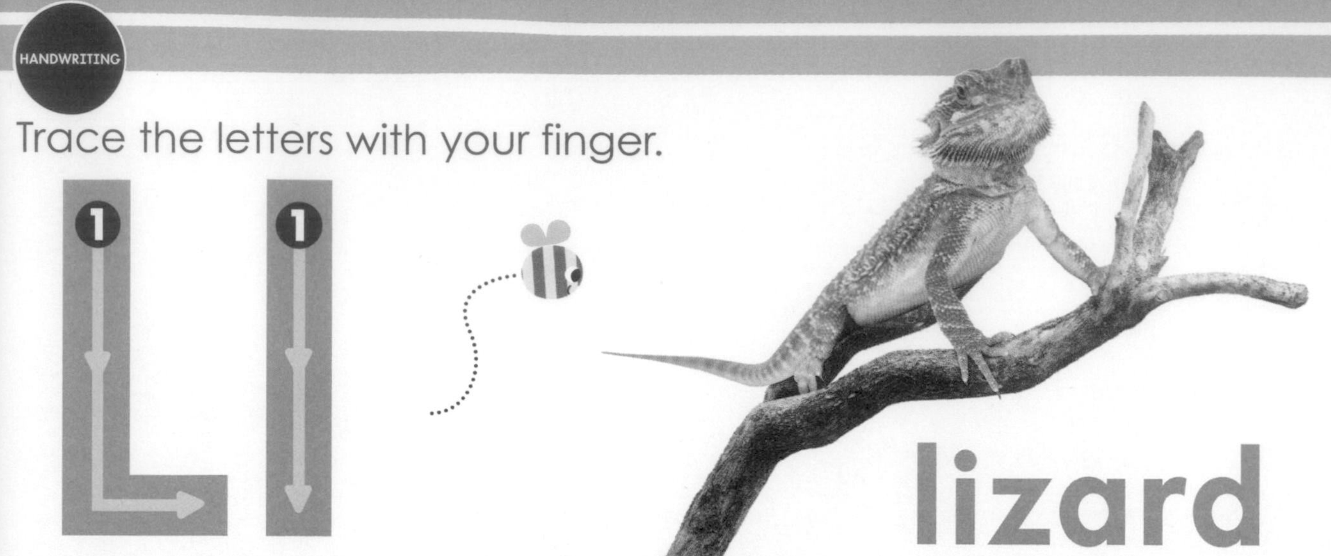

Trace the letters with your pencil.

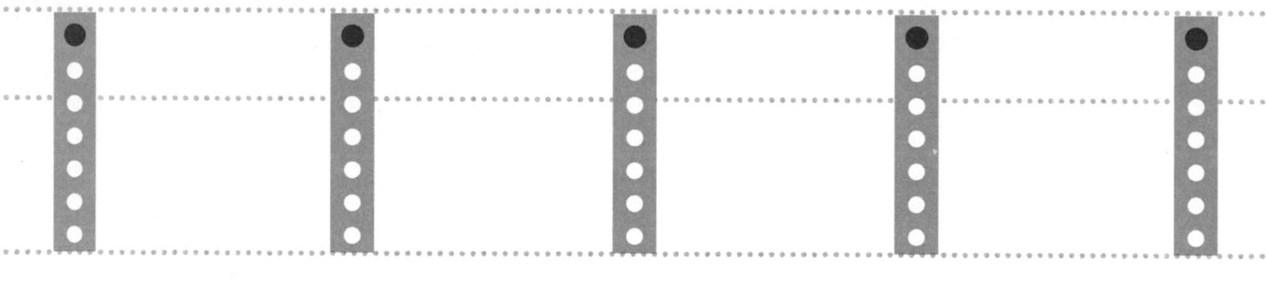

lamp

Trace the letters with your finger.

monster

Trace the letters with your pencil.

m m m m

mouse

Trace the letters with your finger.

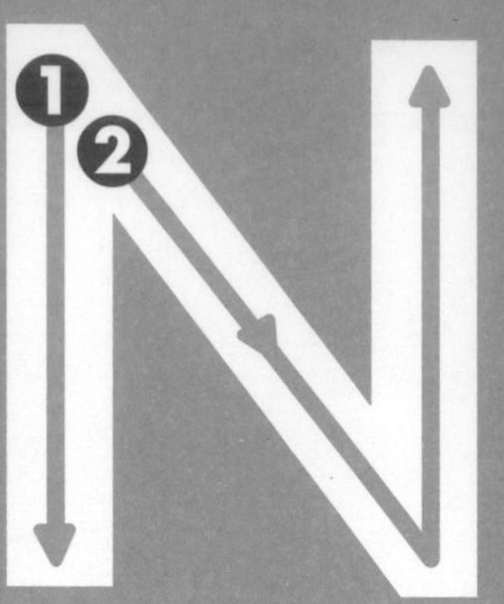

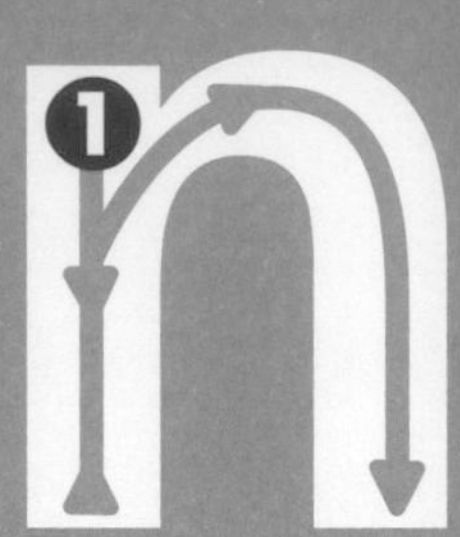

nest

Trace the letters with your pencil.

newt

Trace the letters with your finger.

O o

ostrich

Trace the letters with your pencil.

orange

Trace the letters with your finger.

P p

Trace the letters with your pencil.

P P P P P

p p p p p

Trace the letters with your finger and then with your pencil.

Qq queen

QQQqqq

Rr rabbit

RRRrrr

Trace the letters with your finger.

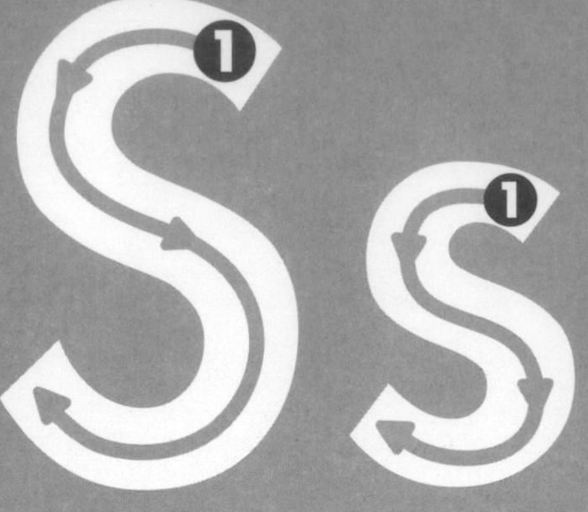

spider

Trace the letters with your pencil.

snake

Trace the letters with your finger.

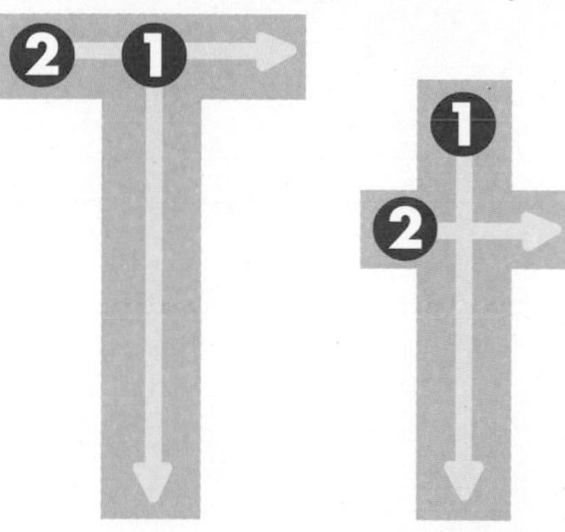

Trace the letters with your pencil.

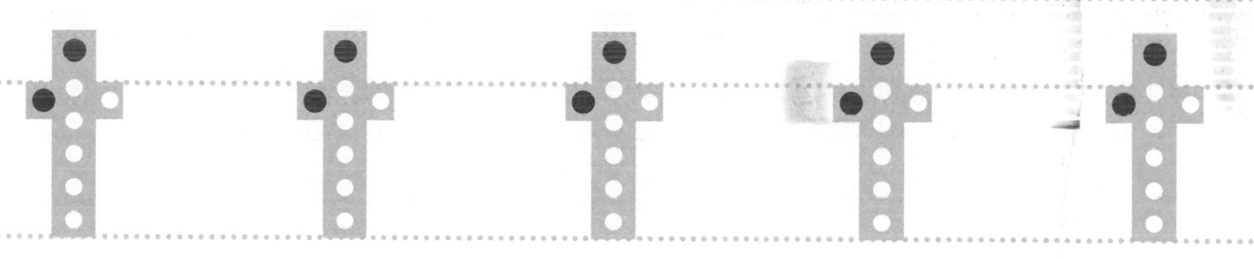

Trace the letters with your finger.

umbrella

Trace the letters with your pencil.

Trace the letters with your finger and then with your pencil.

V v

van

V V V v v v

W w wolf

W W w w

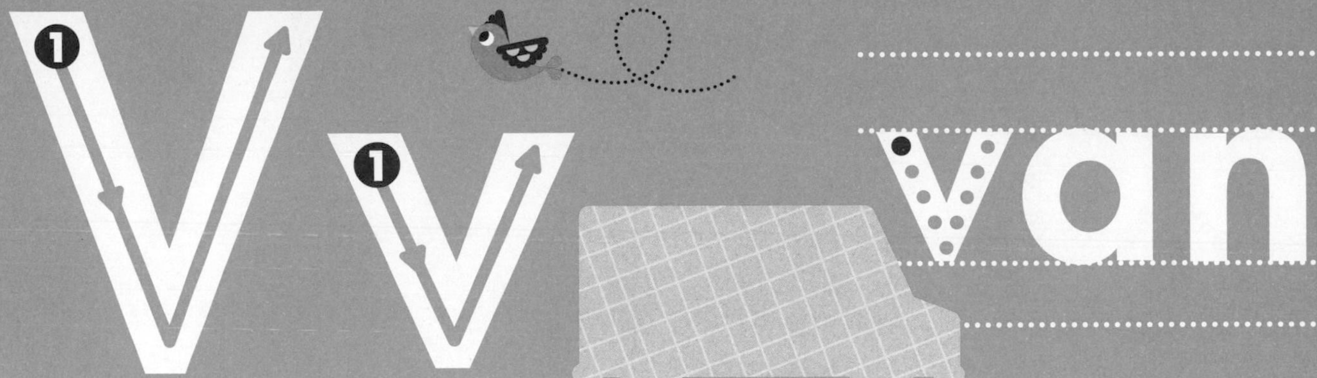

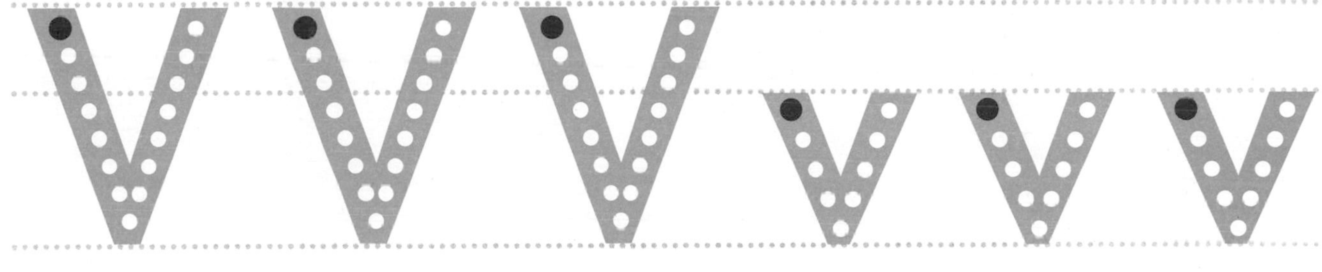

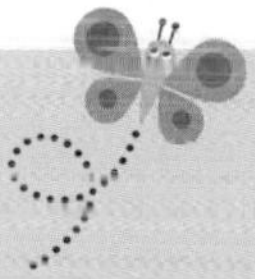

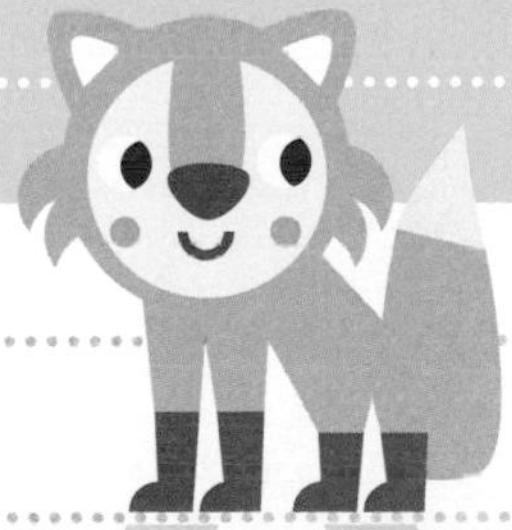

Trace the letters with your finger and then with your pencil.

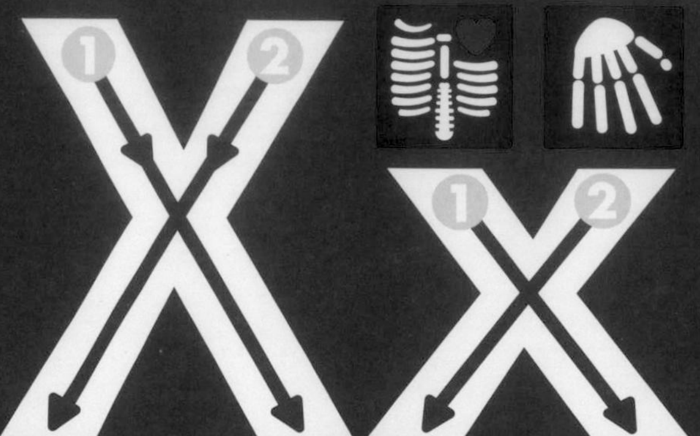

X-ray

yo-yo

Trace the letters with your finger.

Z z

zigzag

Trace the letters with your pencil.

z z z z z

zebra

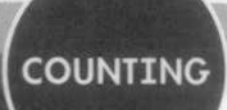

Color the **1**. Then count **1** pig.

one

Trace **1** bow.

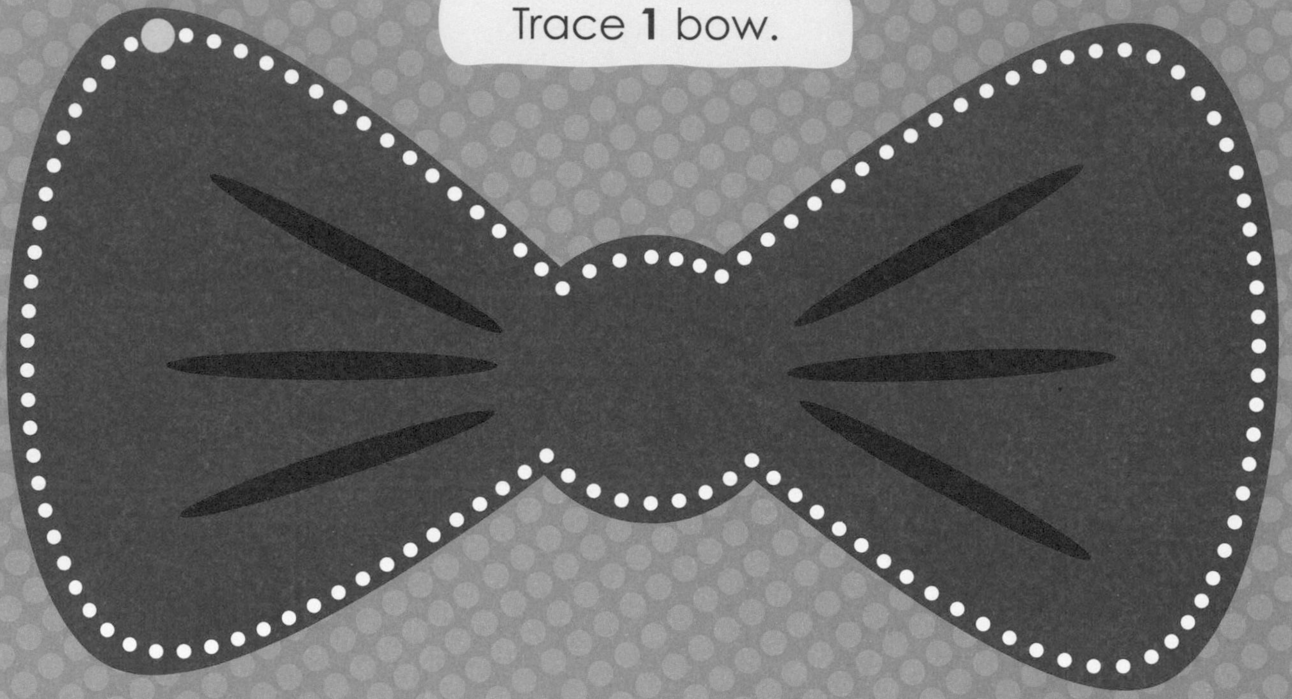

Trace the **1**'s with your finger and then with your pencil.

Color **1** car.

Circle the plate with **1** cupcake on it.

Trace the **2**'s with your finger and then with your pencil.

2 2 2 2 2 2

Count and color **2** butterflies.

Circle the ladybug that has **2** spots.

Color the **3**. Then count **3** strawberries.

three

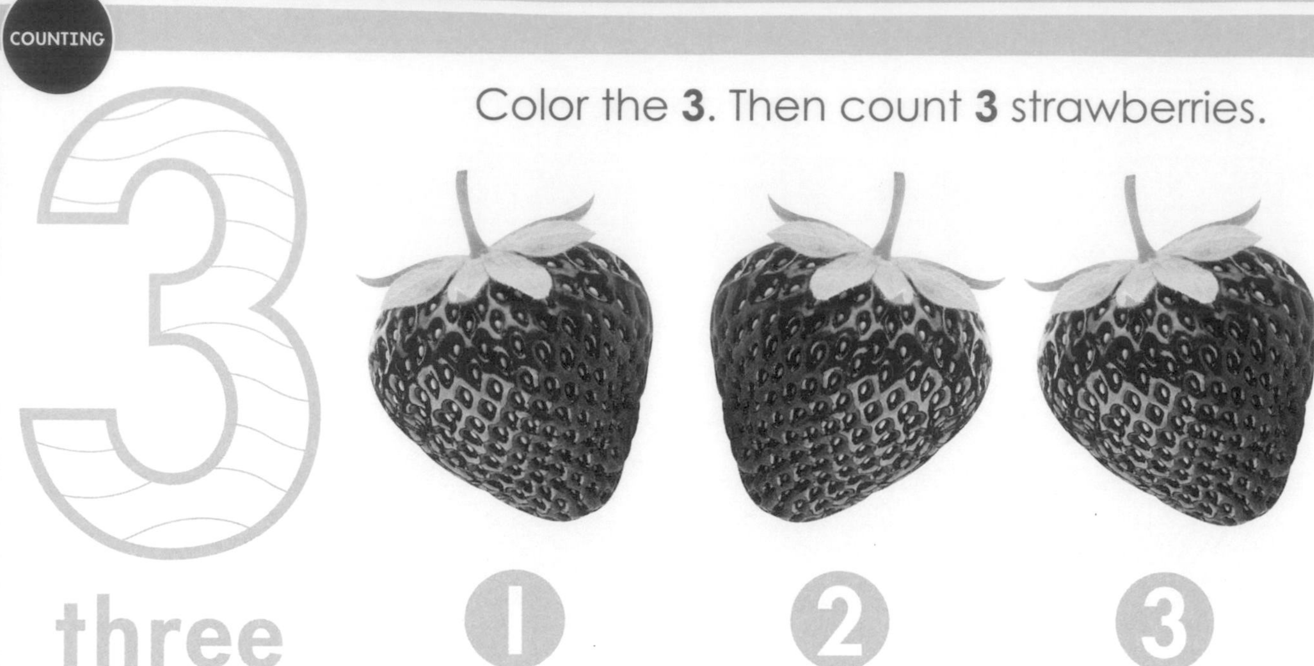

1 2 3

Trace **3** kites.

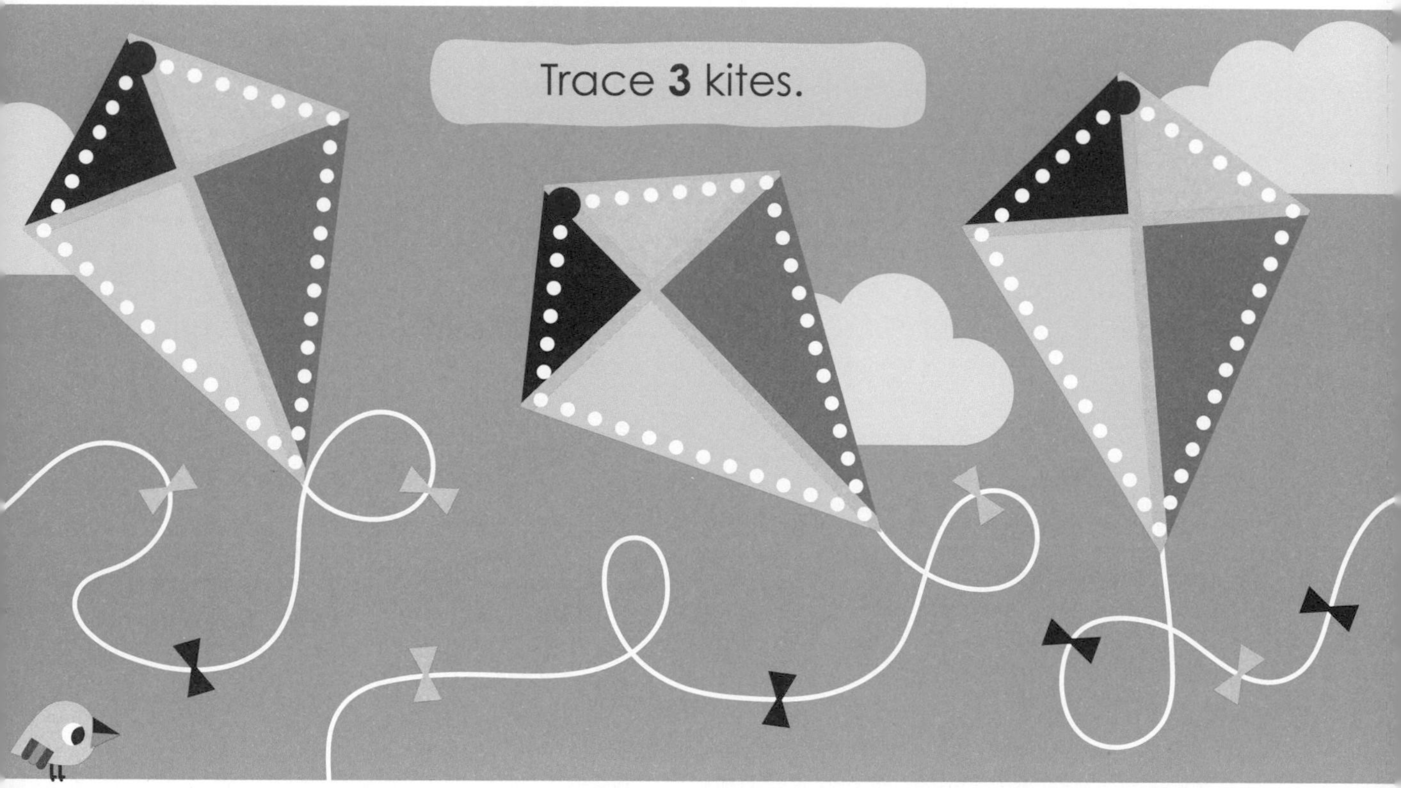

Trace the **3**'s with your finger and then with your pencil.

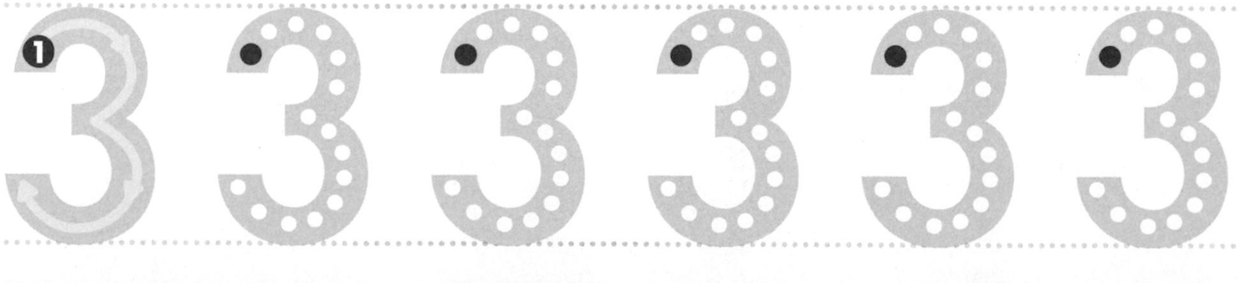

Color **3** fish.

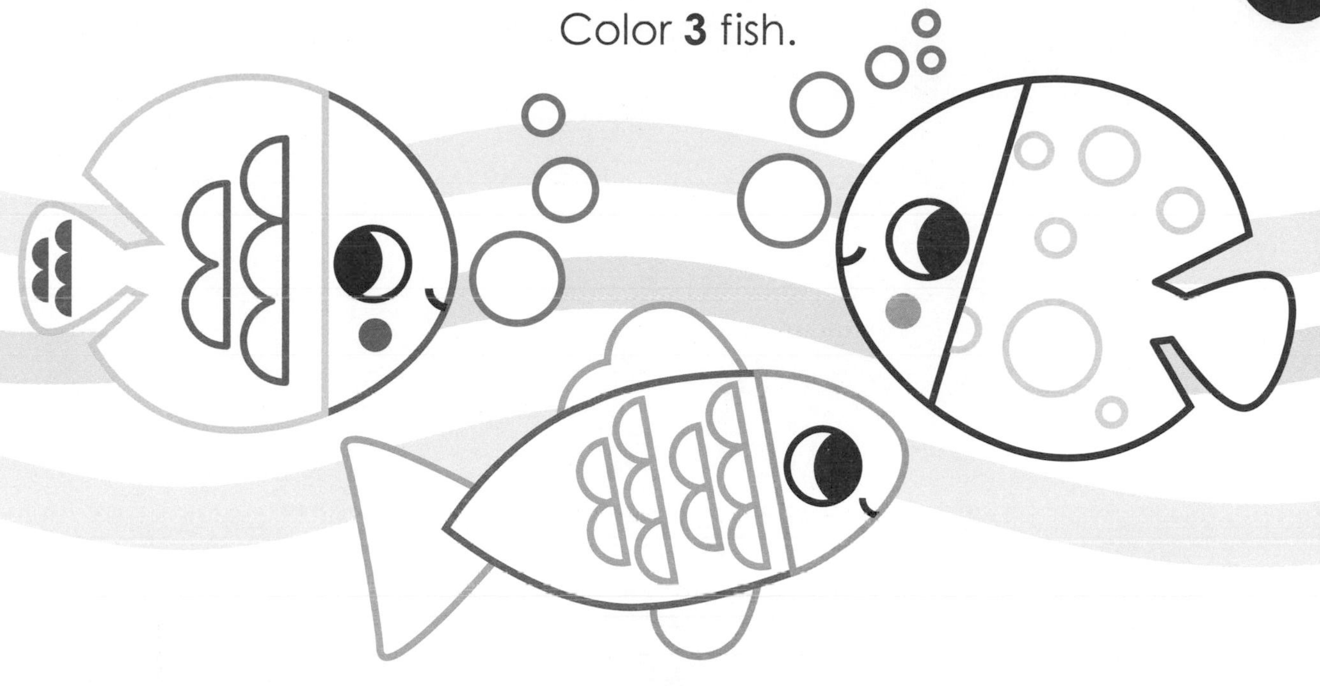

Add **3** stickers to finish the **3** flowers.

Count the cats.

4

four

Color the **4**. Then count **4** trucks.

1 2 3 4

Trace **4** stars.

Trace the **4**'s with your finger and then with your pencil.

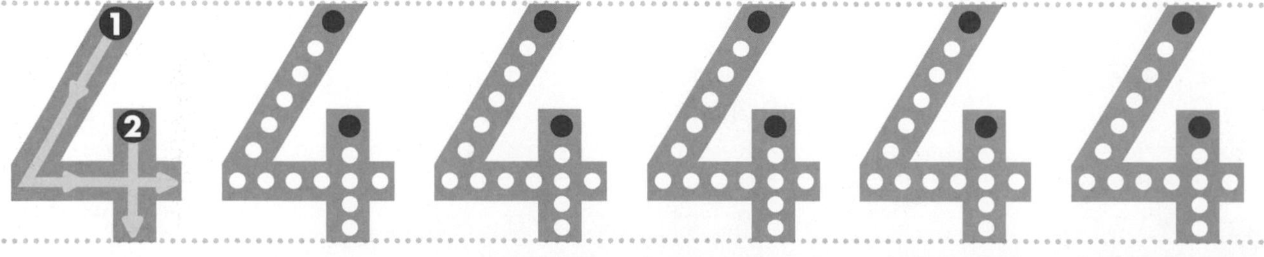

Circle the jar with **4** candies.

Color and sticker **4** beach balls.

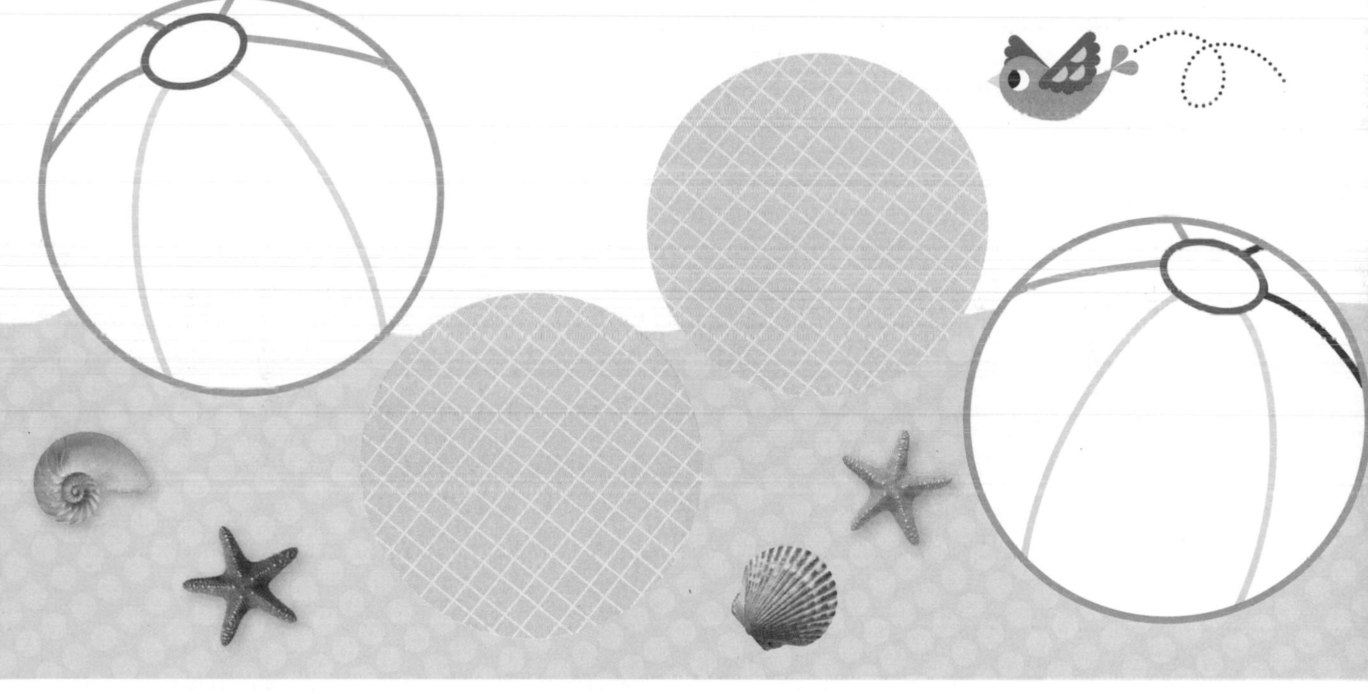

Count the mice.

five

Color the **5**. Then count **5** frogs.

Trace **5** bananas.

Trace the **5**'s with your finger and then with your pencil.

Count the objects in each group.
Then draw lines to match the groups to the numbers.

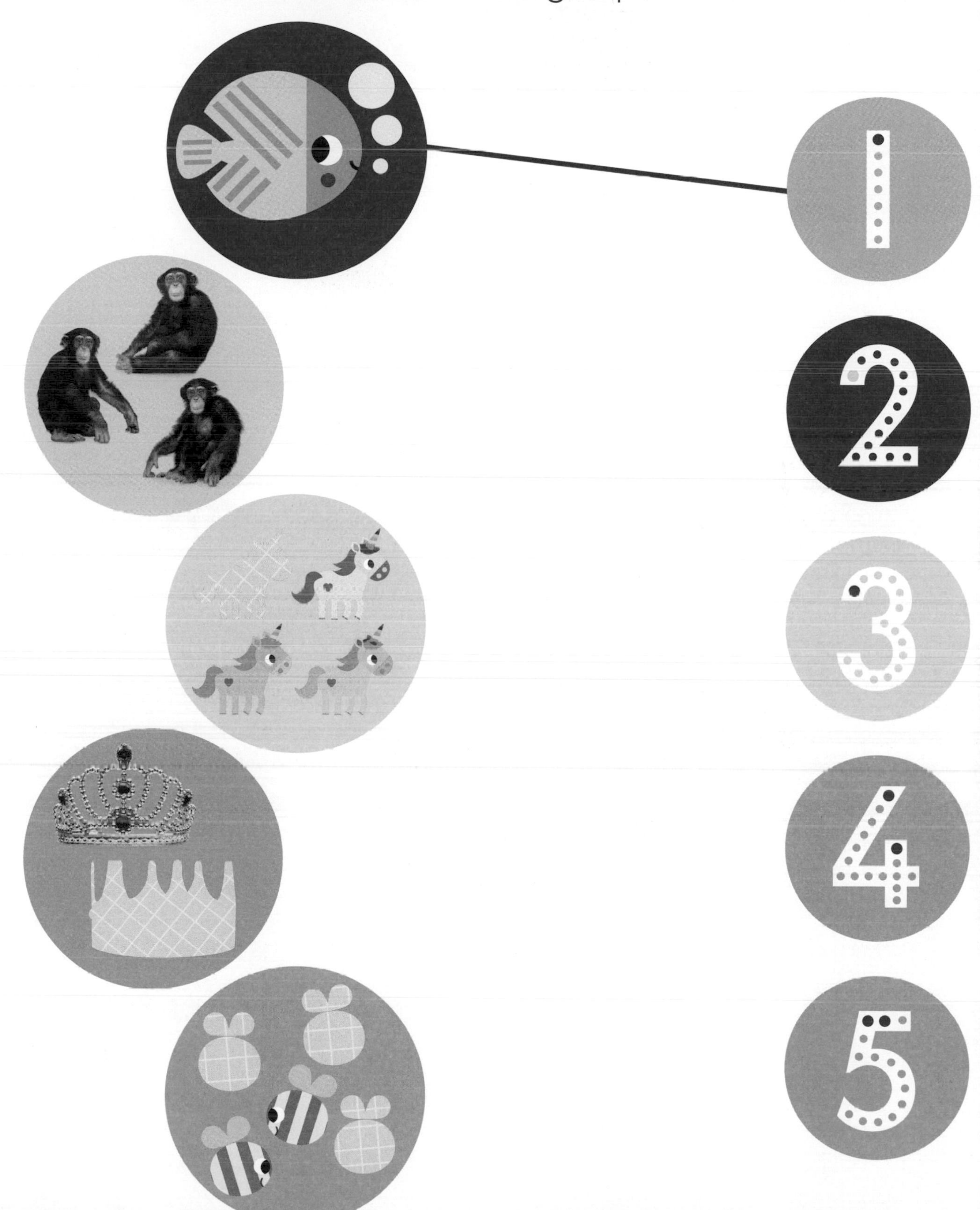

Color the **6**. Then count **6** hats.

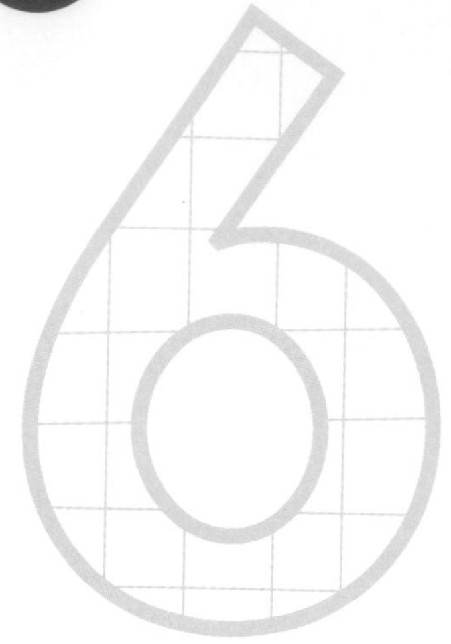

six

1 2 3 4 5 6

Trace **6** buttons.

Trace the **6**'s with your finger and then with your pencil.

Follow the **6**'s to guide the rabbit to its burrow.

seven

Color the **7**. Then count **7** chicks.

Trace **7** shells.

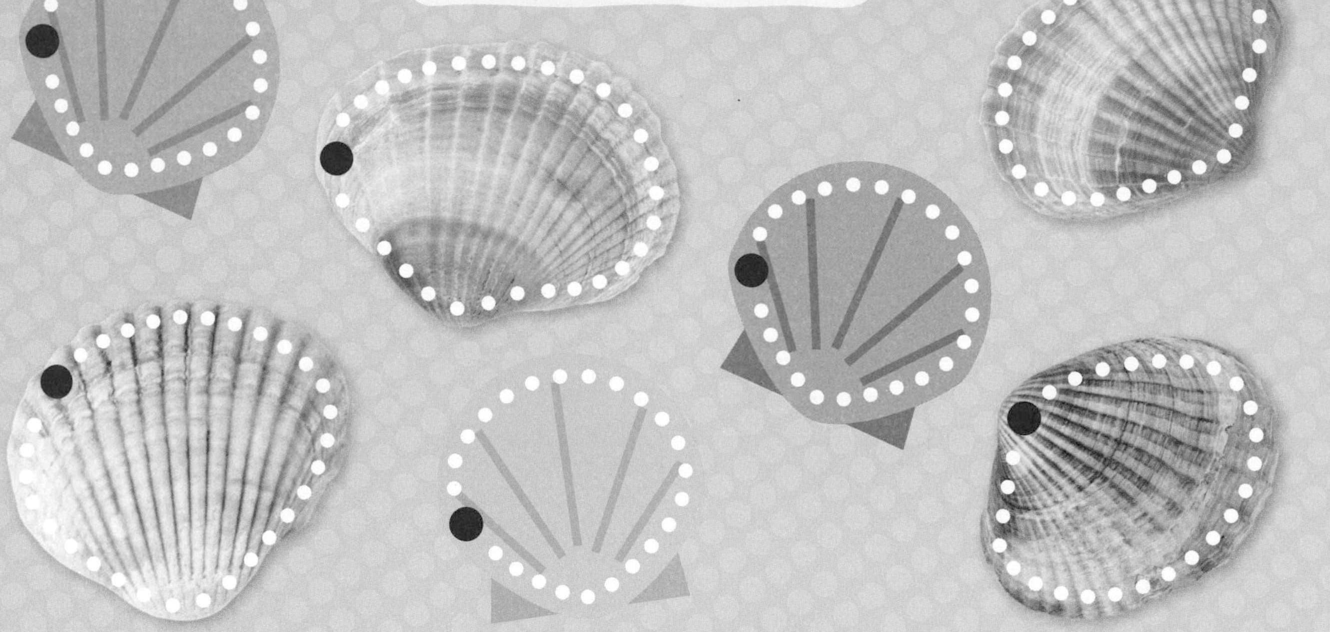

Trace the **7**'s with your finger and then with your pencil.

Circle the tiger with **7** stripes.

Count and color **7** pieces of fruit.

8

eight

Color the **8**. Then count **8** birds.

1 2 3 4

5 6 7 8

Trace **8** yo-yos.

Trace the **8**'s with your finger and then with your pencil.

Count the animals in the zoo.

Add stickers to finish the **8** lollipops.

Color **8** spots on the dog.

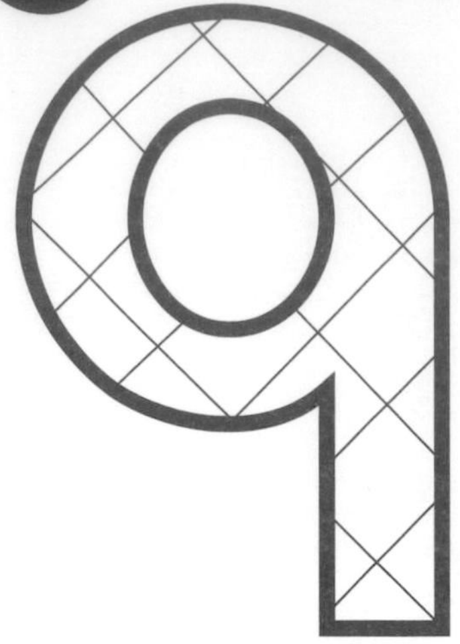

nine

Color the **9**. Then count **9** jewels.

Trace **9** leaves.

Trace the **9**'s with your finger and then with your pencil.

Color **9** gifts.

Trace **9** spikes on the dinosaur's back.

10

ten

Color the **10**. Then count **10** socks.

1 2 3 4 5

6 7 8 9 10

Trace **10** cookies.

Trace the **10**'s with your finger and then with your pencil.

10 10 10 10

Count the objects in each group.
Then draw lines to match the groups to the numbers.

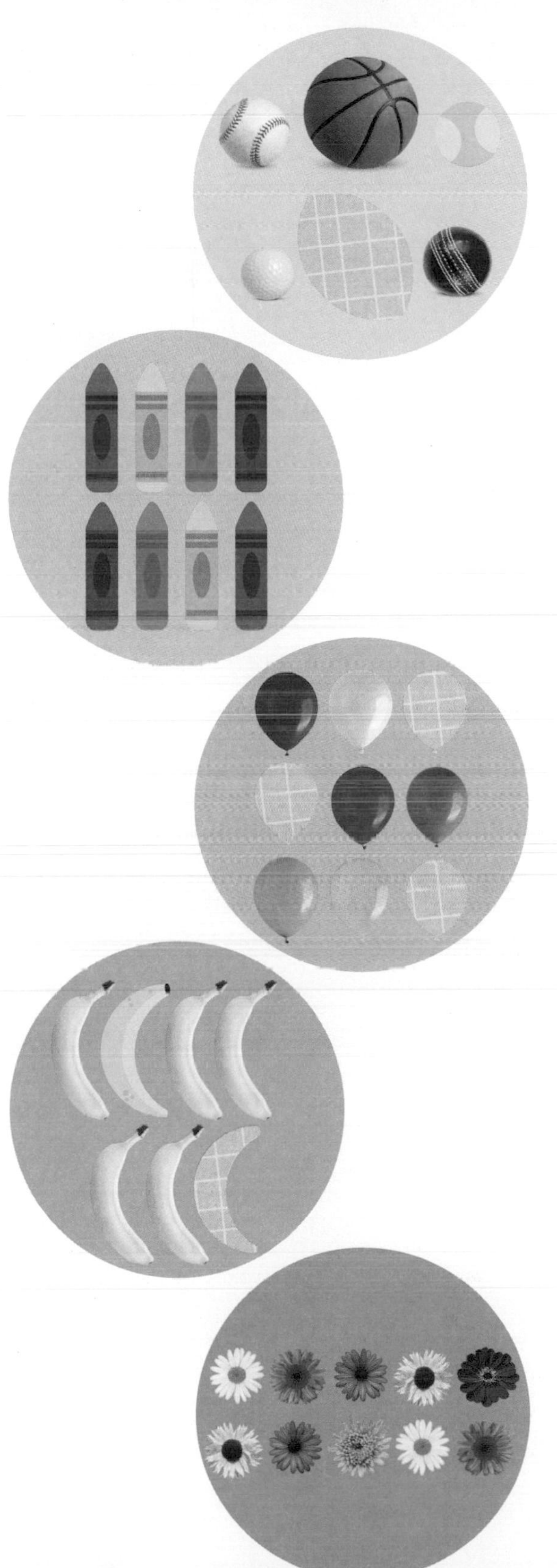

What's different?

Circle the picture that is different.

Circle the picture that is different.

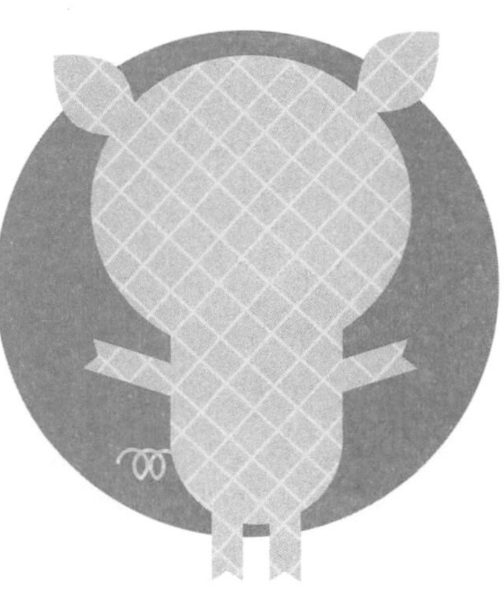

What's different?

Circle the picture that is different.

Circle the picture that is different.

What's different?

Circle the bear that is different.

Circle the tricycle that is different.

What's different?

Circle the puppy that is different.

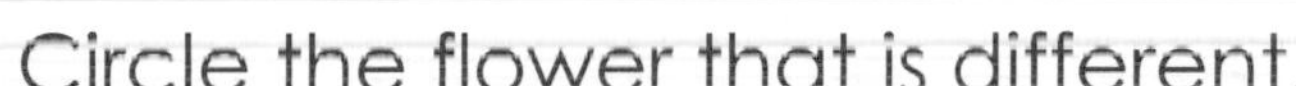

Circle the flower that is different.

Make them different

Give the yellow emoji a happy smile.
Give the **blue** emoji a sad mouth.

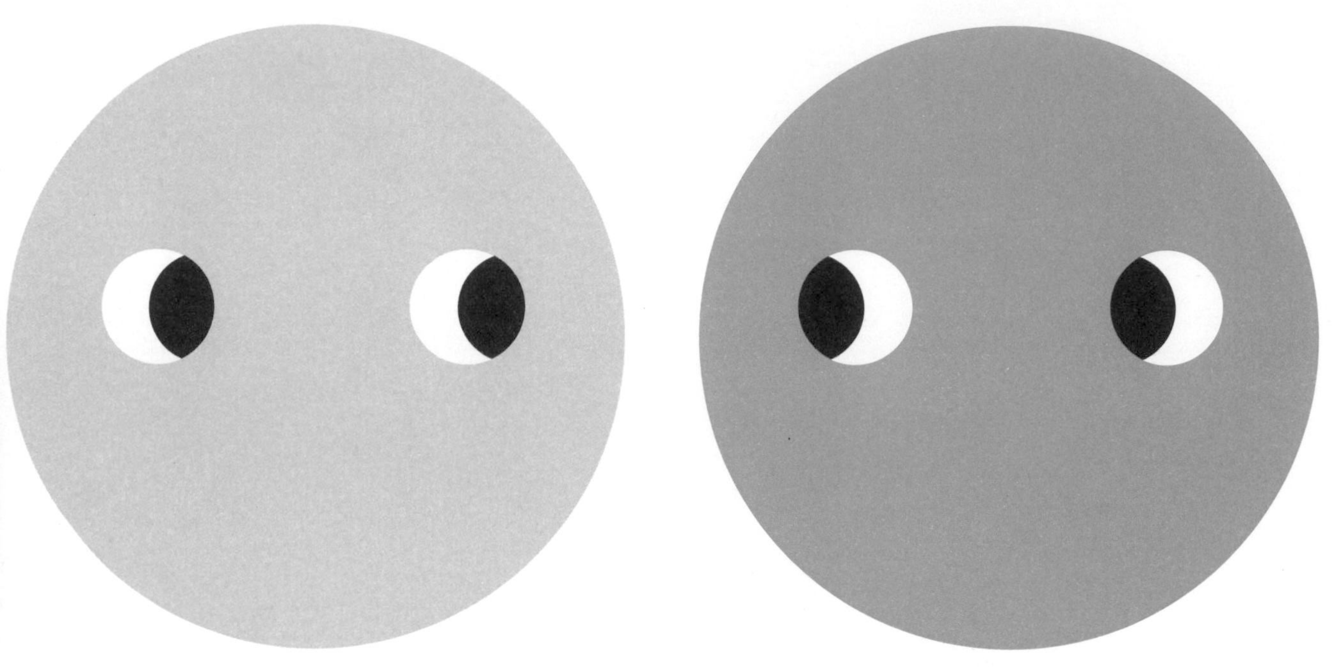

Color the buses different colors.

Make them different

Give one dinosaur **red** spots.
Give the other dinosaur **blue** spots.

Color the girls' clothes different colors.

Looking the same

Circle the rabbits that are the same.

Color the other tractor the same colors as this one.

Find the pair

Circle the button that is the same as this one.

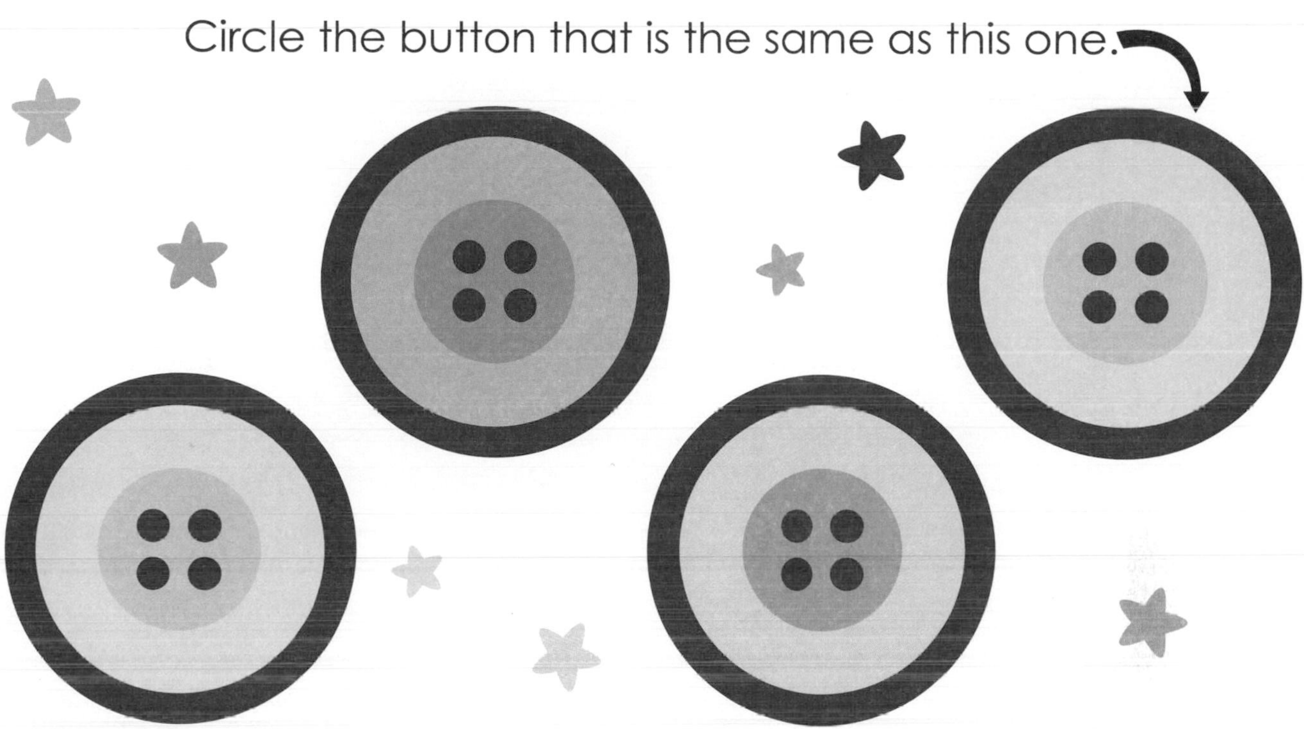

Circle the shell that is the same as this one.

Match the pairs

Draw lines to join the pictures that are the same.

Match the pairs

Draw lines to join the pictures that are the same.

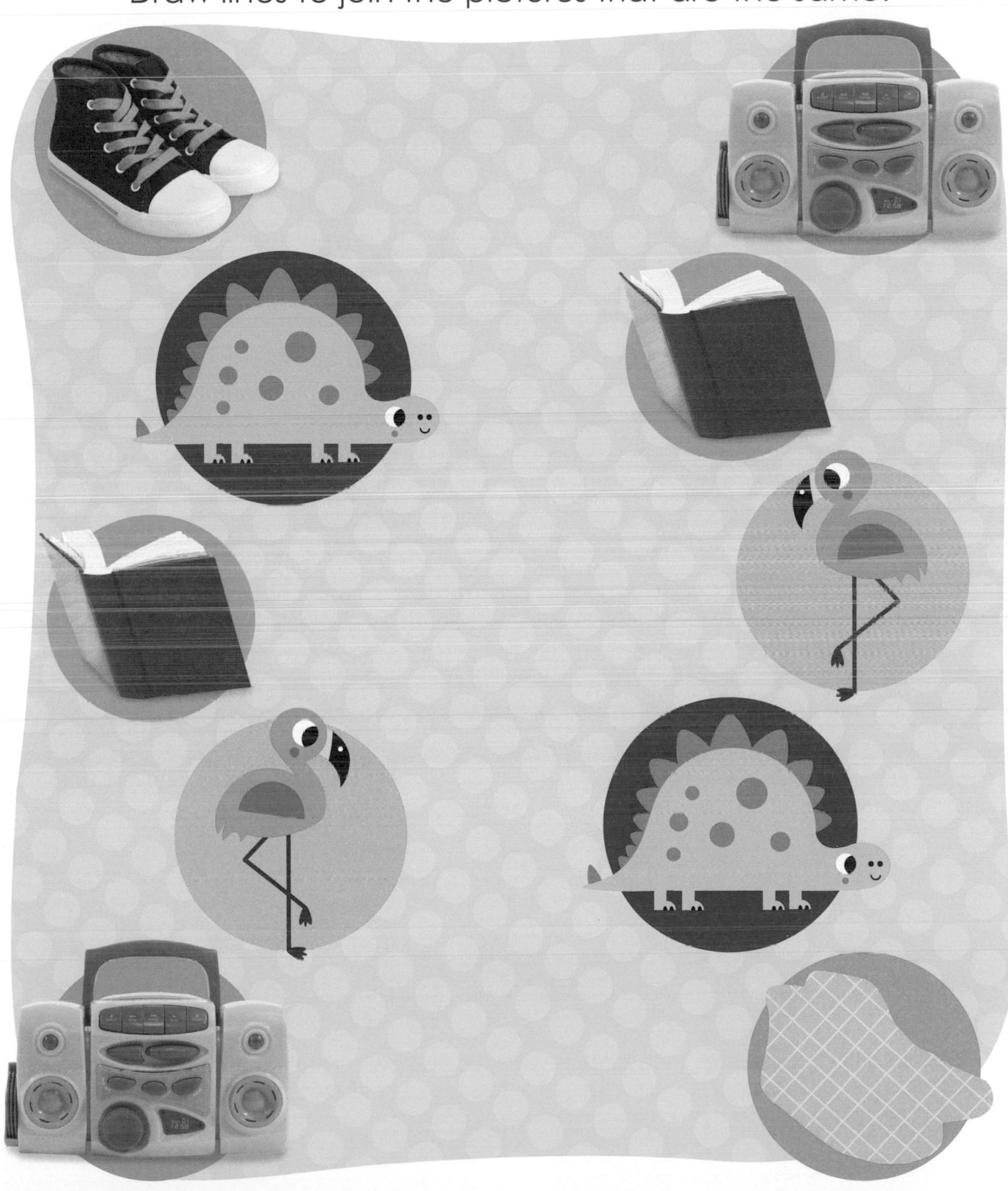

Put them away

Draw a line from each building brick to the box with its matching color.

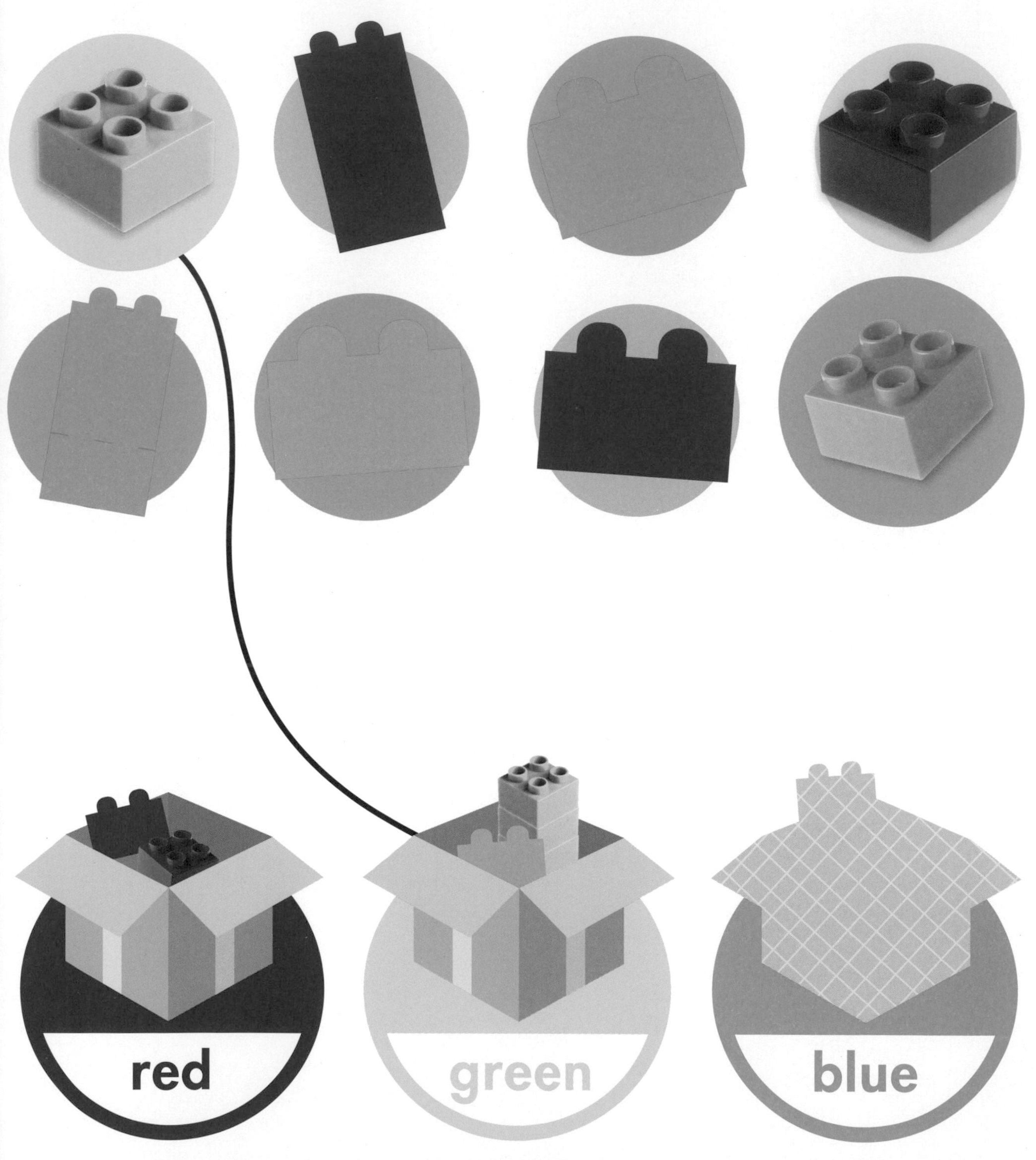

Put them away

Draw lines from the knives, forks, and spoons to the correct trays.

Match the size

Circle the cone with the same amount of ice cream as this one.

Circle the tree that is the same size as this one.

Match the height

Circle the boy who is the same height as this one.

Circle the giraffe that is the same height as this one.

Find the biggest

Circle the biggest bunch of flowers.

Circle the tallest girl.

Find the smallest

Circle the smallest butterfly.

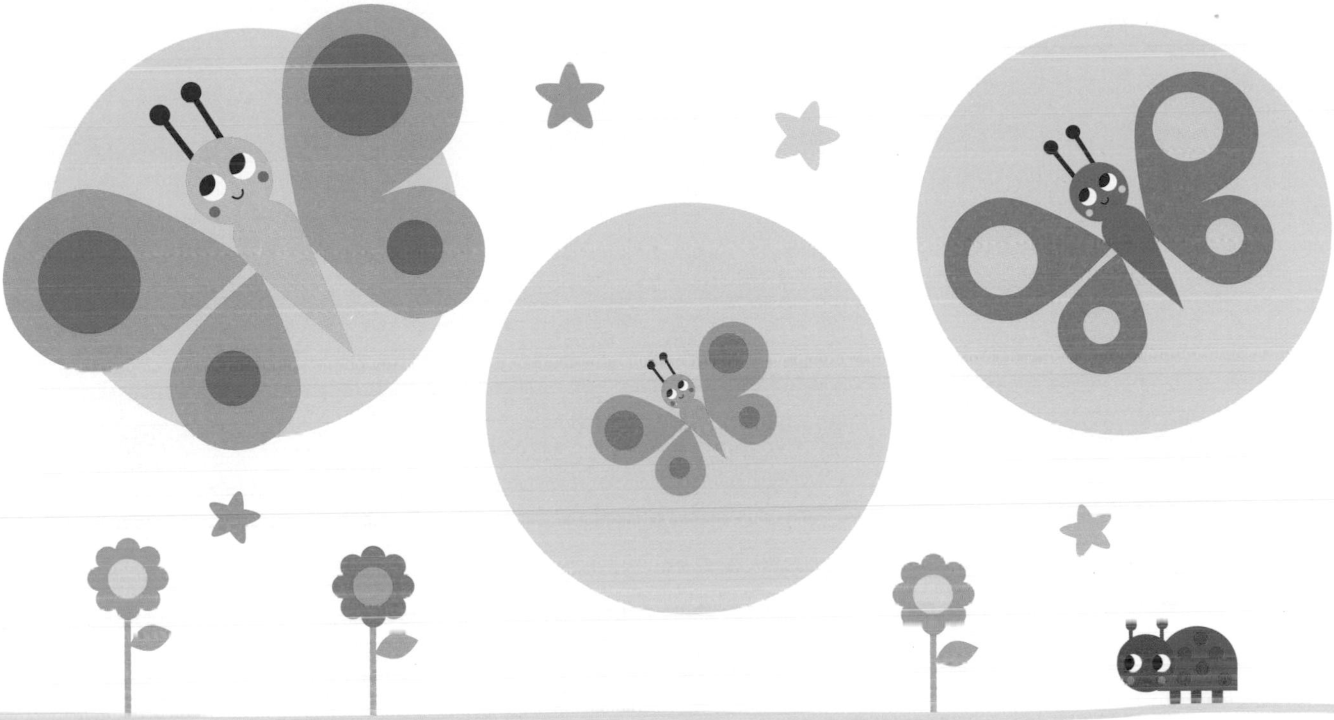

Circle the shortest dog.

Find the difference

Circle the monkey that is upside down.

Circle the picture that is upside down.

Find the difference

Circle the child who is facing the other way from the others.

Circle the fish that is facing the other way from the others.

Animals grow

Look at the growing kitten.
Circle the picture where he is the youngest.

What comes first? Sticker the numbers 1 to 3 in order.

Plants grow

Look at the growing plant.
Circle the picture where it is the oldest.

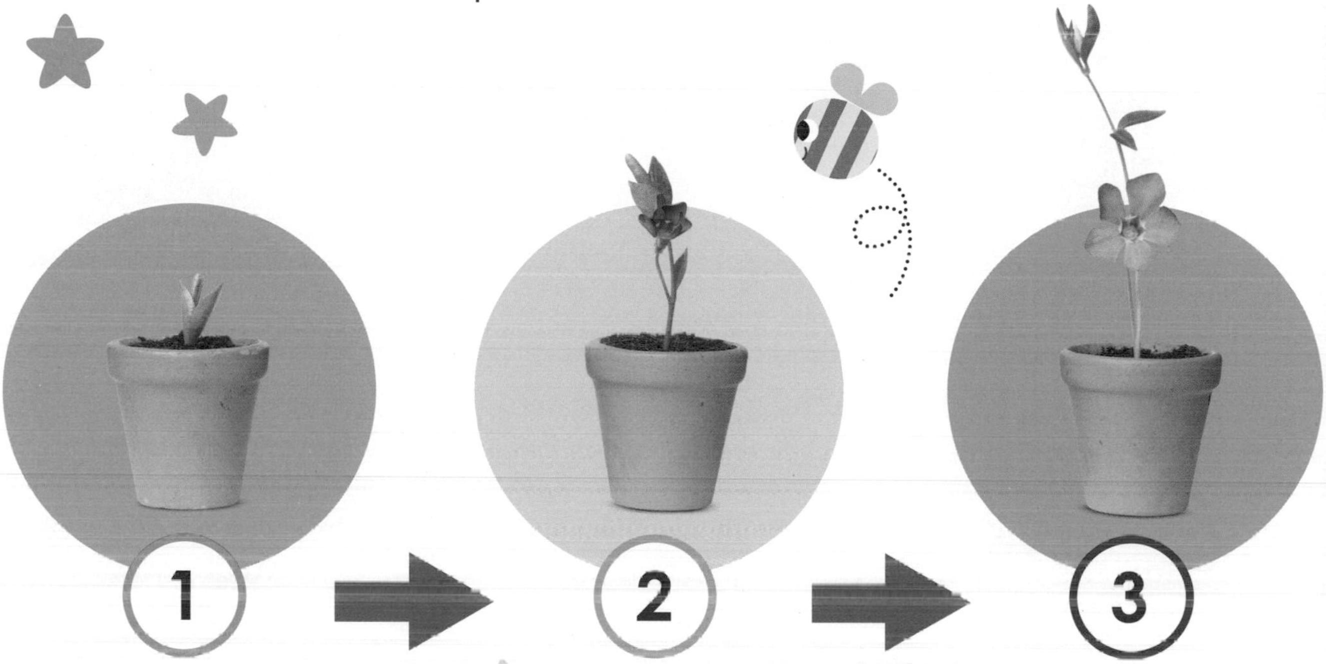

1 → 2 → 3

What comes first? Sticker the numbers 1 to 3 in order.

Plants we eat

Much of the food we eat comes from plants.
Draw lines to match the plant with the food.

What animals eat

Some animals eat plants and some eat meat.
Draw lines from the animals to the things they eat.

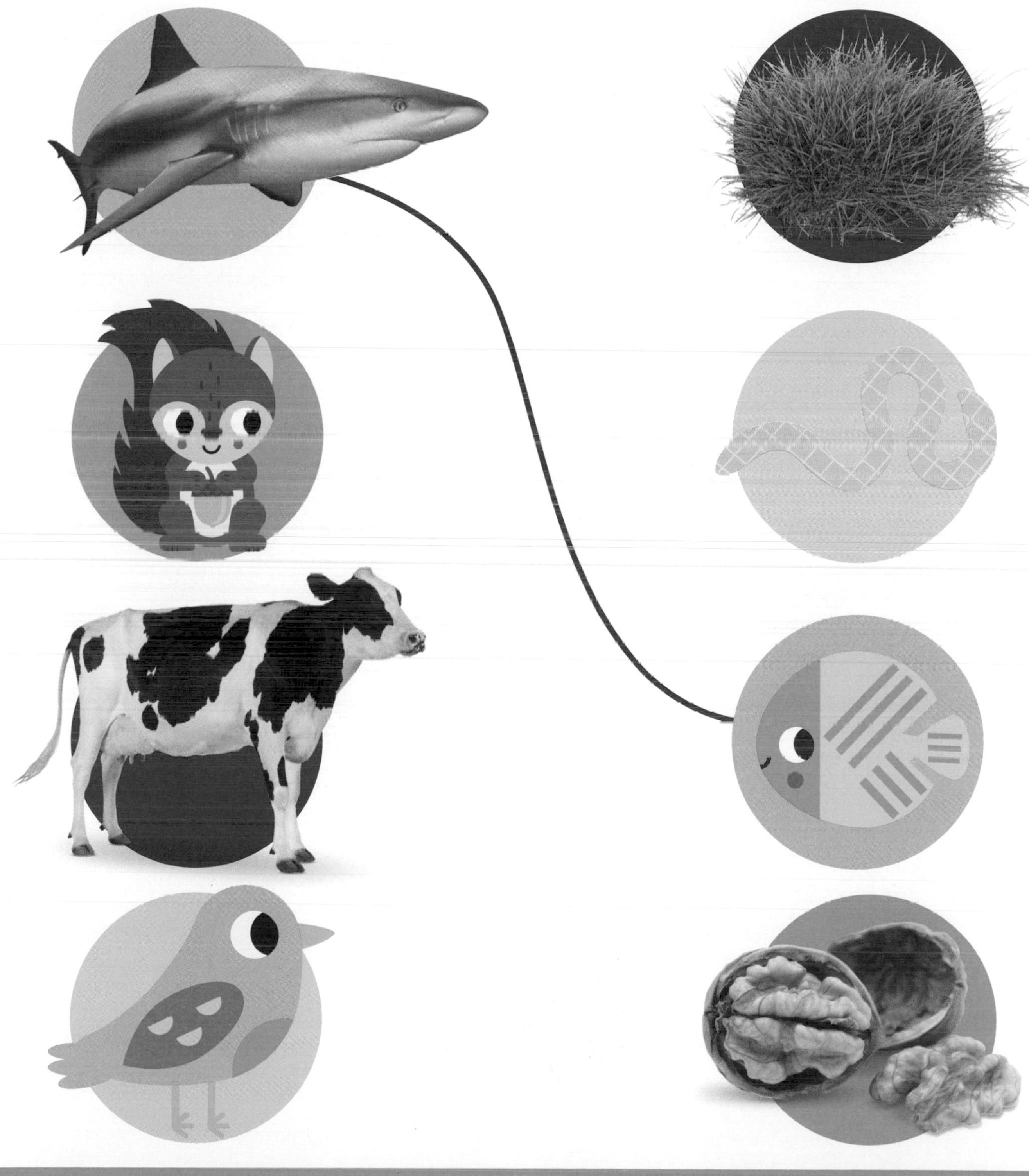

Fur, feathers, and scales

Sticker the rabbit with the other furry animals.

Sticker the snake with the other scaly animals.

Sticker the parrot with the other feathered animals.

Animal homes

Draw lines to match the animals with their homes.

Leaf shapes

Different trees have differently shaped leaves.
Draw lines to match the leaves.

pine needles

oak leaf

holly leaf

maple leaf

Pretty flowers

Draw lines to match the flowers.
Color the flowers on the right to match the ones on the left.

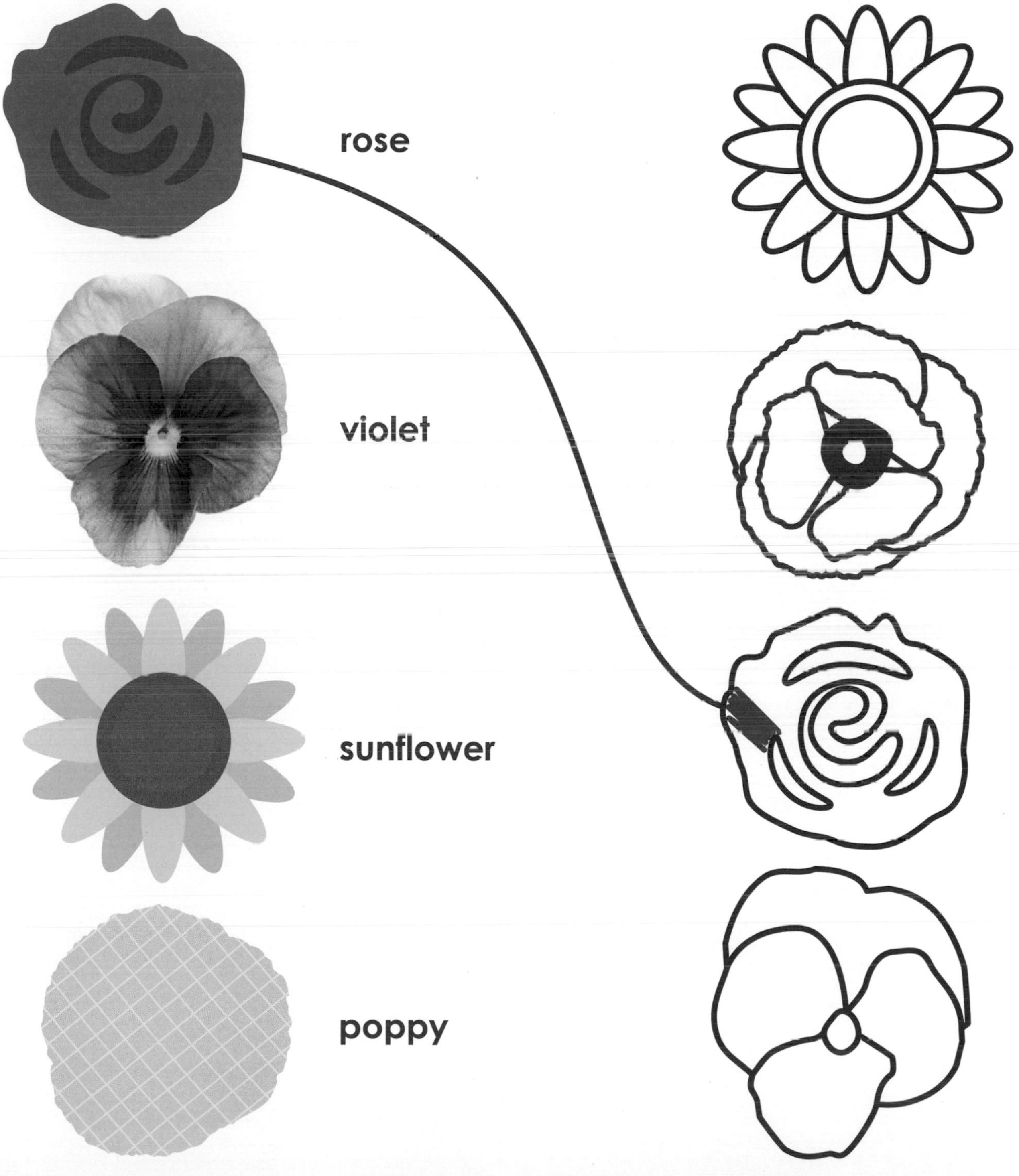

rose

violet

sunflower

poppy

Day and night

Sticker the animals we see during the day in the daytime scene.

Sticker the animals we see at night in the nighttime scene.

Shadows

Shadows form in places where light cannot reach.
Draw lines to match the animals with their shadows.

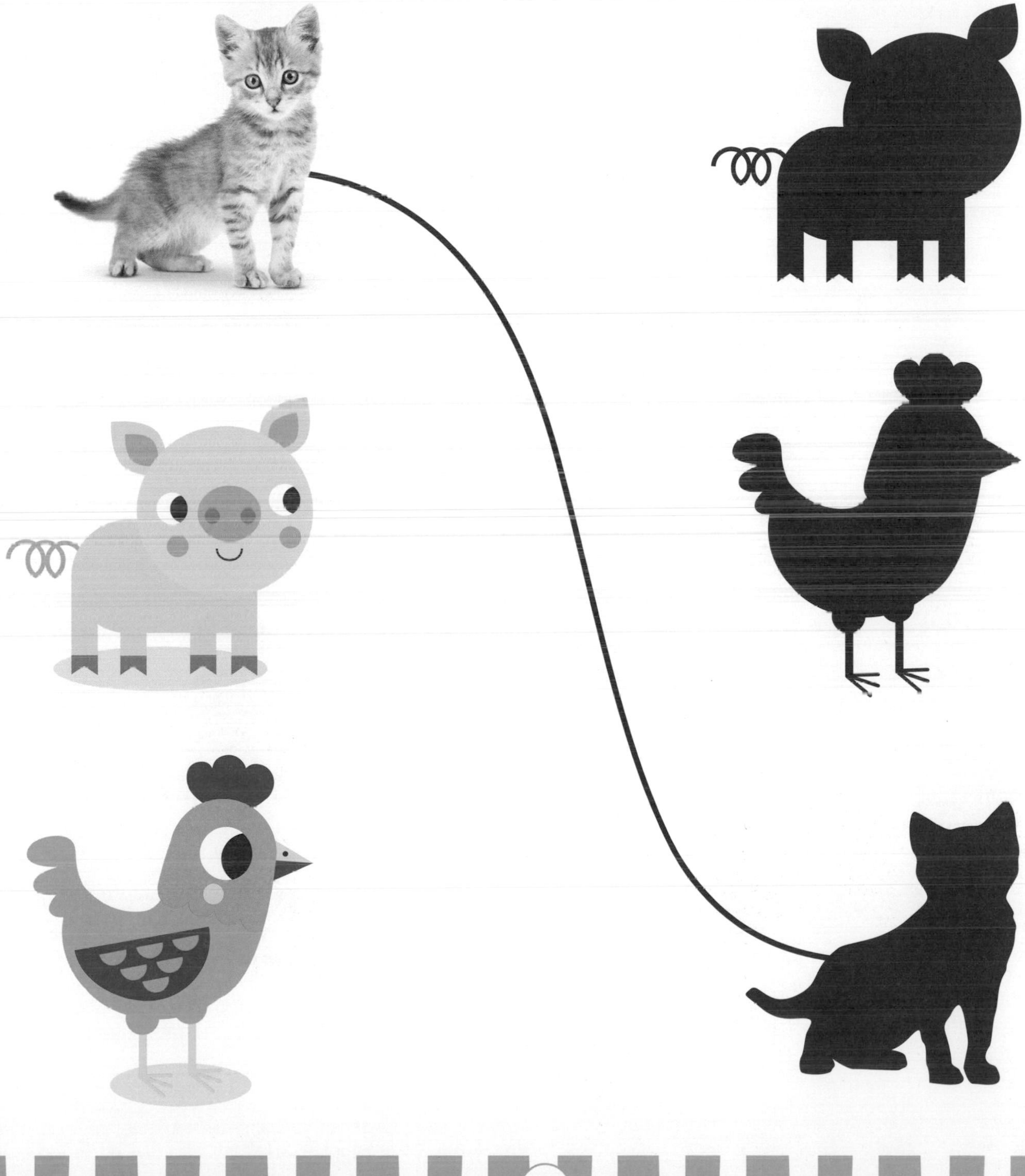

Seasons

Sticker the correct season name into each scene.

A tree through the year

Trees change with the seasons.

Sticker **blossoms** on the spring tree.

Sticker **apples** on the summer tree.

Sticker a **snowman** under the winter tree.

Sticker **colorful leaves** on the fall tree.

Weather

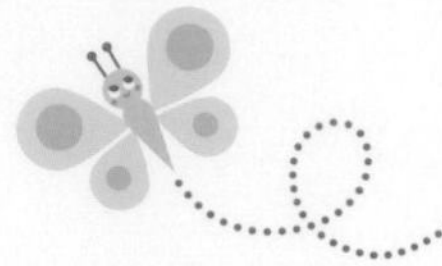

Trace the raindrops in the rainy scene.

Trace the sun's rays in the sunny scene.

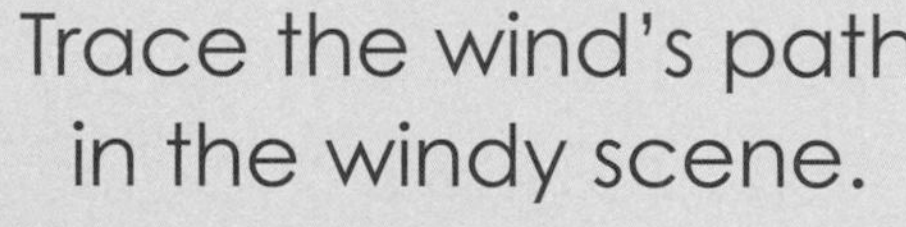

Trace the snowflakes in the snowy scene.

Trace the wind's path in the windy scene.

Rainbows

Rainbows form when the sun shines through raindrops.
Color the rainbow's stripes the same colors as the dots.

Heavy or light?

Sticker a brick by the things that are heavy.
Sticker a feather by the things that are light.

Fast or slow?

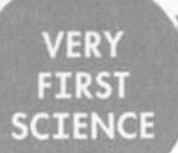

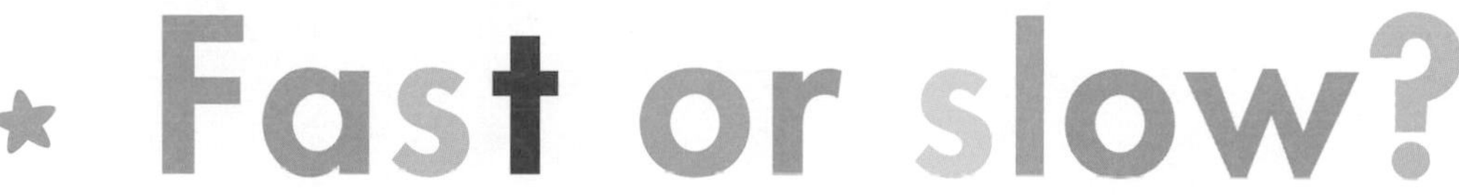

Some things move fast. Some things move slowly.
Circle the things that move fast.

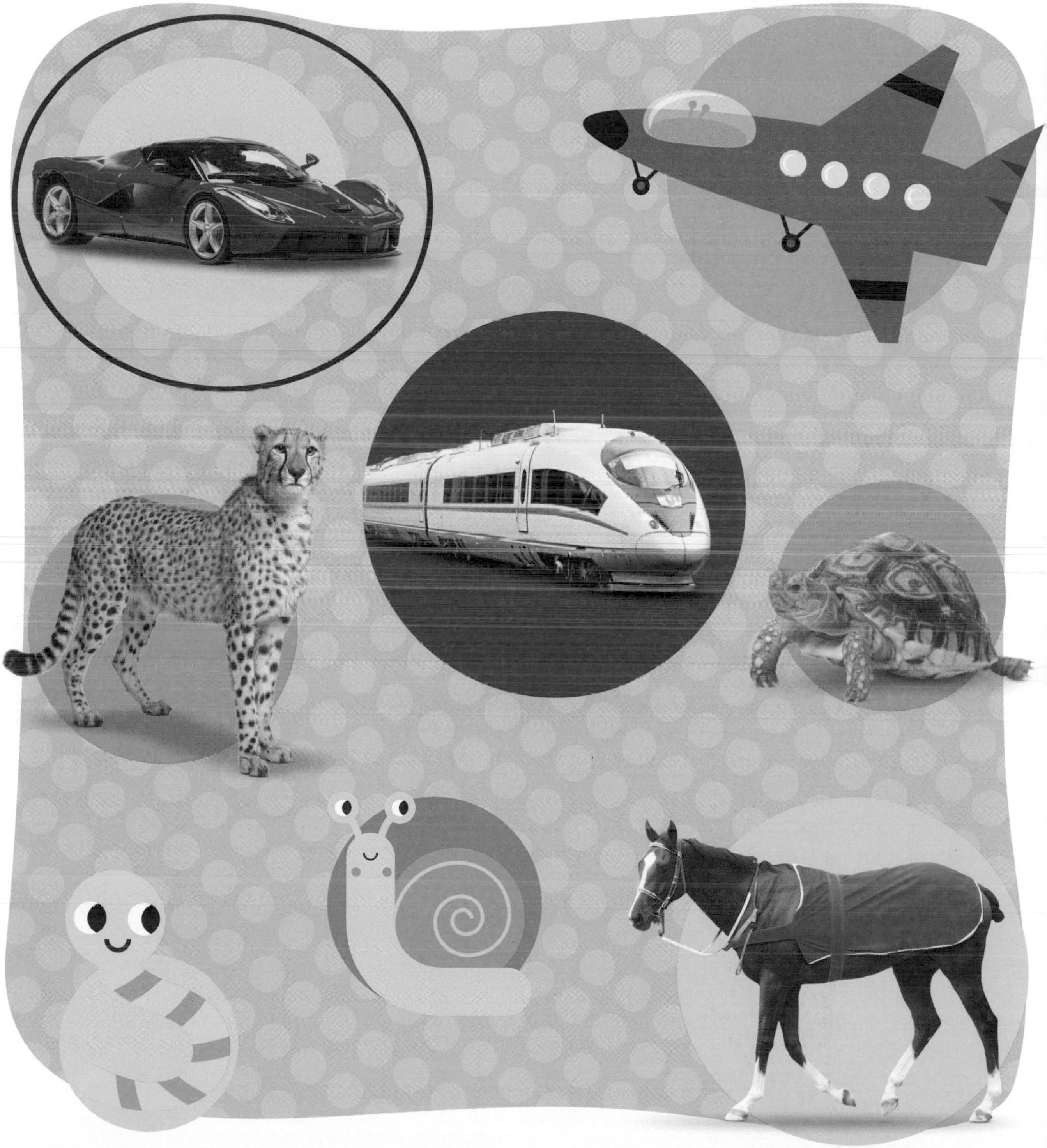

Push or pull?

Circle the things we push with a **blue** pencil.
Circle the things we pull with a **red** pencil.

Is it stretchy?

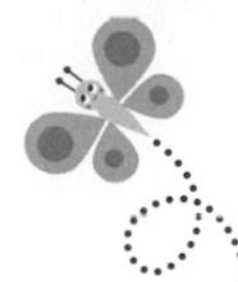

Some things stretch when we pull them. Other things do not.
Circle the stretchy things.

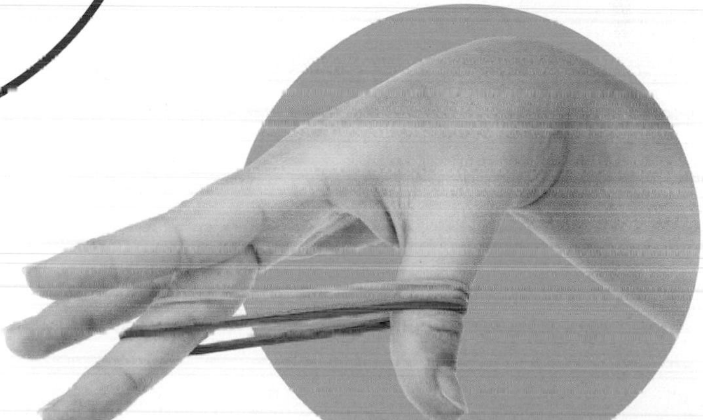

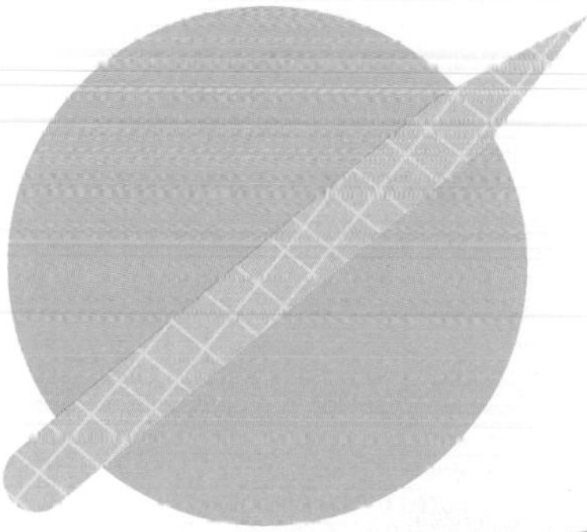

Jobs people do

Name the jobs. Then circle all the ones that you'd like to do.

doctor

teacher

barber

letter carrier

baker

farmer

storekeeper

mechanic

To the rescue!

Draw lines to connect the emergency workers with their jobs.

police officer

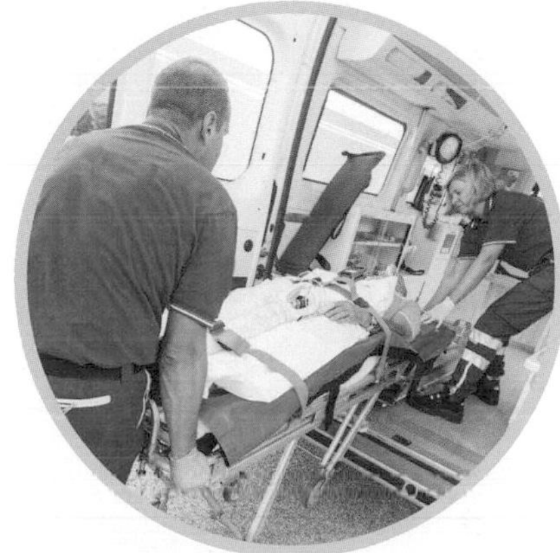

helping sick people

firefighter

helping lost children

paramedic

firefighting

On the road

Name the vehicles.
Then circle the ones you've seen on roads near you.

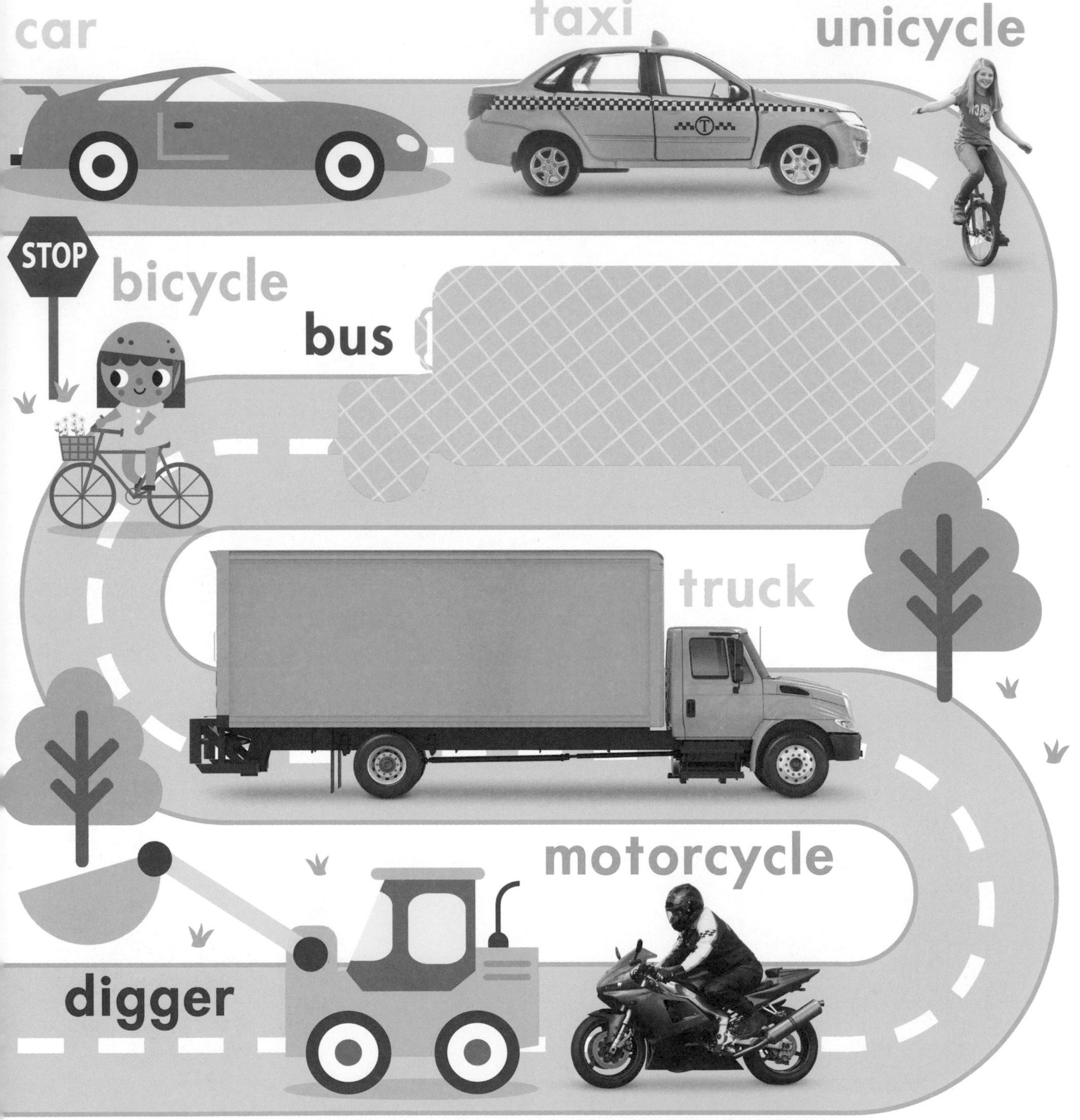

car

taxi

unicycle

STOP

bicycle

bus

truck

motorcycle

digger

In the sky

Name the vehicles.
Then circle the ones you've seen in the sky above you.

hot-air balloon

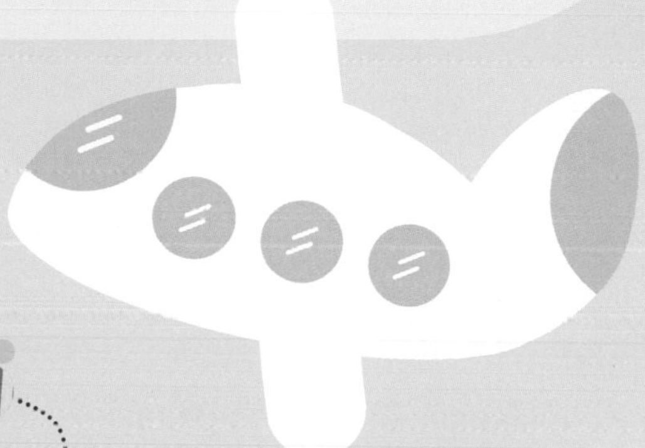

airplane

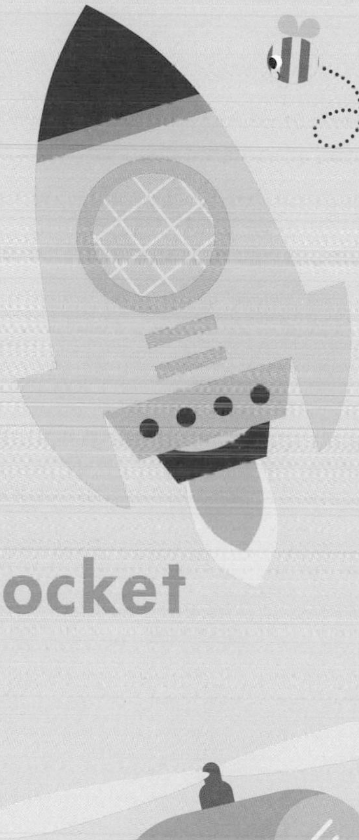

rocket

parachute

hang glider

helicopter

In the city

Cross out the things that don't belong in the city.

In the country

Cross out the things that don't belong in the country.

In the forest

Find, name, and circle all the animals in this forest scene.

In the ocean

Find, name, and circle all the sea creatures in this ocean scene.

Keeping fit

Draw lines to join the equipment with the activity.

soccer ball

swimming

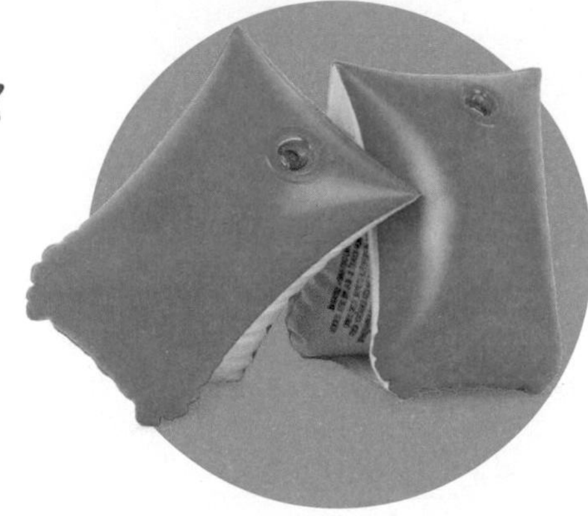

water wings

biking

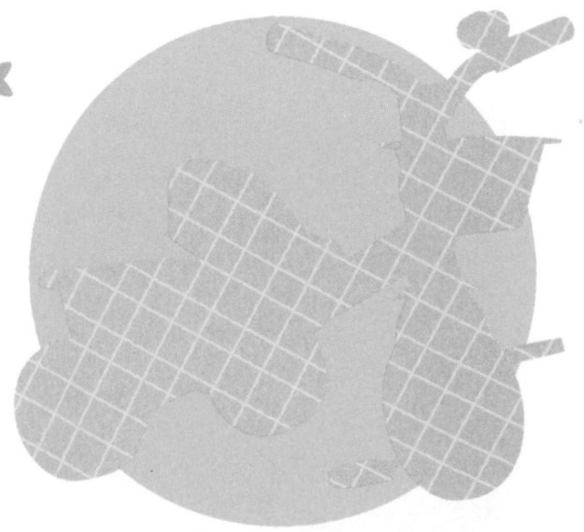

tricycle

playing soccer

Fun activities

Draw lines to join the equipment with the activity.

pencils

sliding

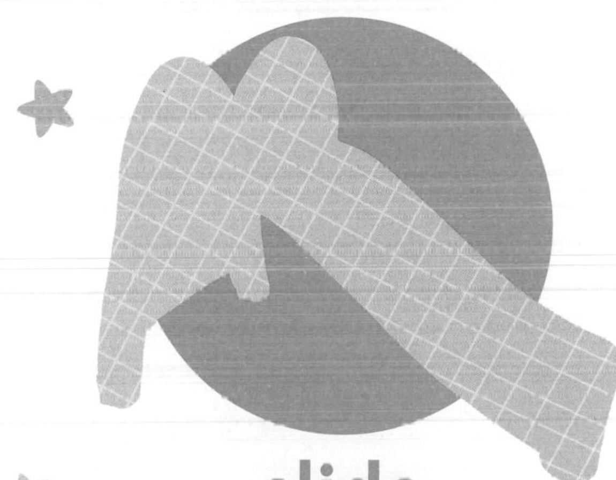

slide

reading

book

drawing

Going shopping

Draw lines to join the objects with the stores where we buy them.

shoes

teddy bear

dog bed

At the supermarket

Name the foods. Then circle the ones that your family buys.

eggs

MILK

milk

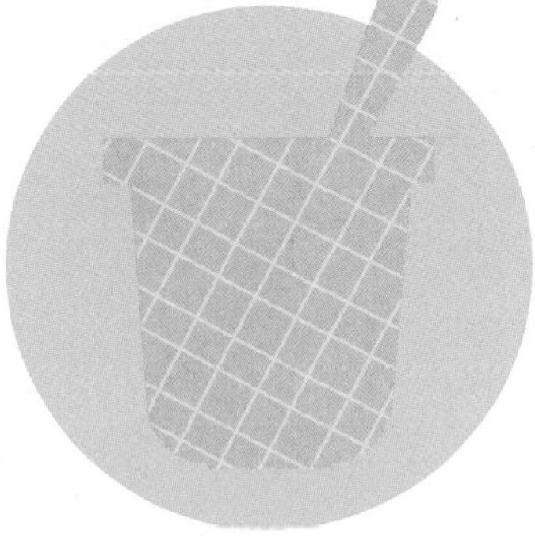

yogurt

cereal

apples

carrots

corn

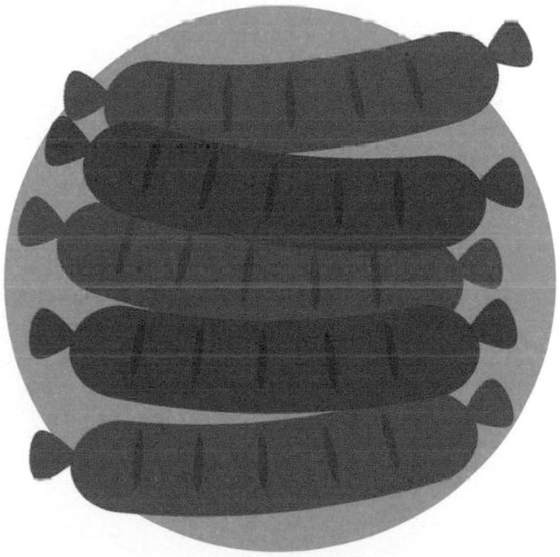

sausages

Keeping safe

Circle the things that help keep you safe.
Cross out the things that are dangerous.

running with scissors

wearing a seatbelt

wearing a bike helmet

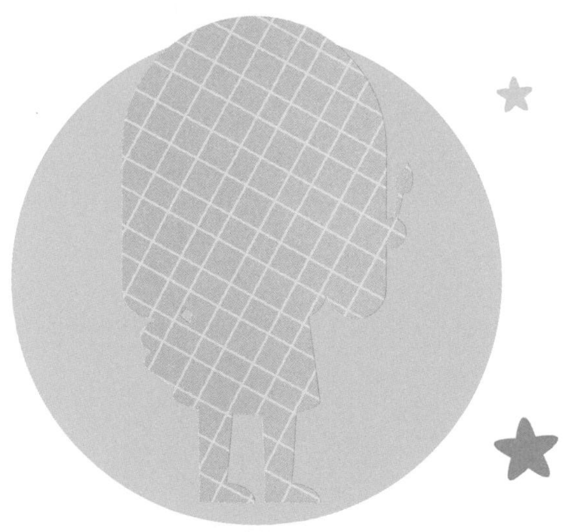

playing with matches

Crossing the road

Circle the things that help keep you safe.
Cross out the things that are dangerous.

looking both ways

using a crosswalk

crossing with an adult

running into the road

Who can help?

Circle the people who you can ask for help.

a baby

parents

a police officer

a teacher

All about me

If I get lost, I can tell people who I am.

My name is

....

My phone number is

....

I live at

....

....

....

More about me

Circle all the things that describe you.

I am a girl.

I have curly hair.

I am a boy.

I like trucks.

I like animals.

I have straight hair.

My picture

Here are some children. Draw yourself with the children.

Time for preschool

Let's go to preschool!
Circle the things you say when you get to preschool.
Cross out the things that would be silly to say.

Good morning!

Hi!

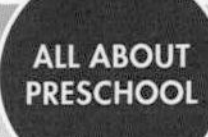

Monkeys!

How are you?

Bananas!

Hello!

At preschool

At preschool, you might have a cubby.
Color and sticker this cubby picture.

Draw lines from the cubby to the things that you can store in your cubby.

coat

cow

backpack

helmet

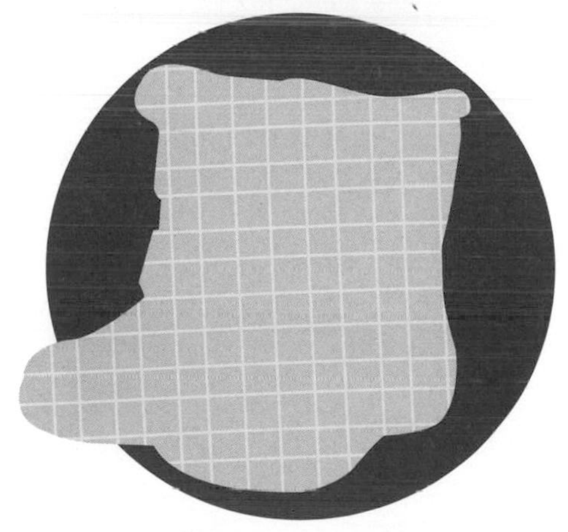

piano

boots

Playing inside

Sometimes you will play inside.
Circle the playtime activities.
Cross out the things you don't do at playtime.

sleeping

reading

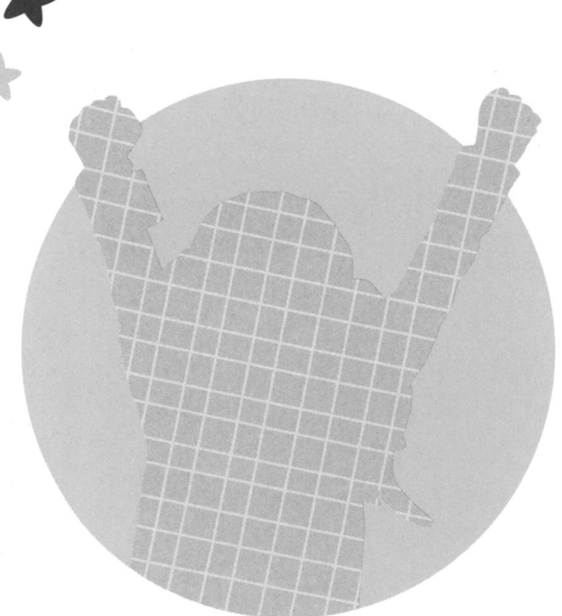

dressing up

taking a bath

building

playing with trains

painting

doing a jigsaw puzzle

Story time

A teacher might read you a story.
Color and sticker this story-time picture.

What do you do when the teacher is reading?
Circle the correct picture.

talk to friends

listen to the story

How do you ask a question? Circle the correct picture.

put up your hand

shut your eyes

Snack time

Circle the things you might eat and drink at snack time.
Cross out the things you do not eat.

yogurt

bowl

hat

sandwich

apple

milk

chair

fruit juice

Nap time

At preschool, you might take a nap.
Sticker and color the nap-time picture.

Wash your hands

Draw lines from the girl washing her hands to the times when you should wash your hands.

after using the bathroom

after reading

before eating

after getting dirty

Making things

Match the things you use to make things with the pictures of children using them.

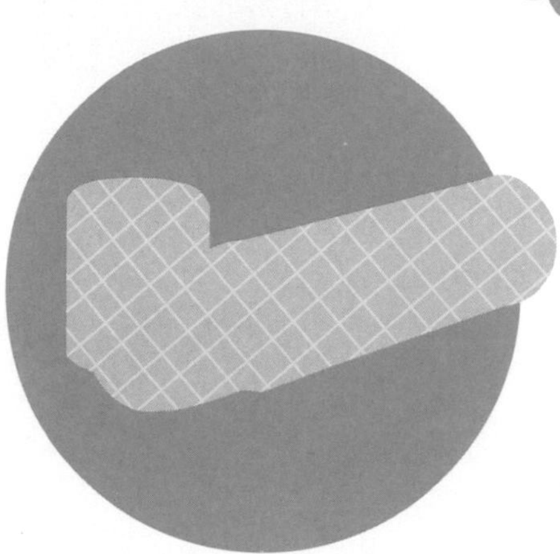

glue stick

drawing

crayons

sticking

cutting out

modeling clay

molding

painting

paints

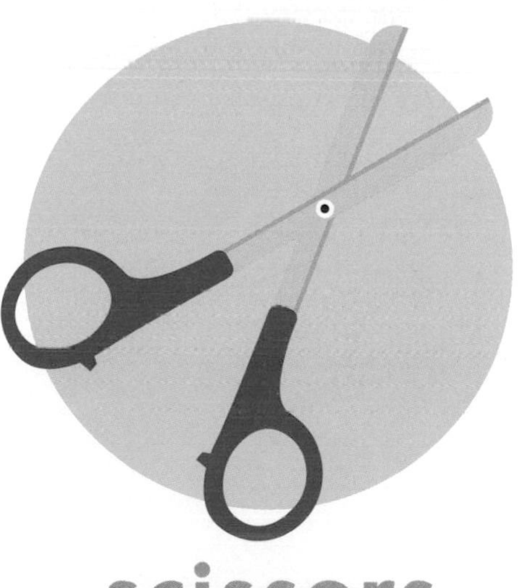

scissors

Making music

Match the musical instruments with the people using them.

drum

playing the recorder

recorder

playing a drum

piano

playing the xylophone

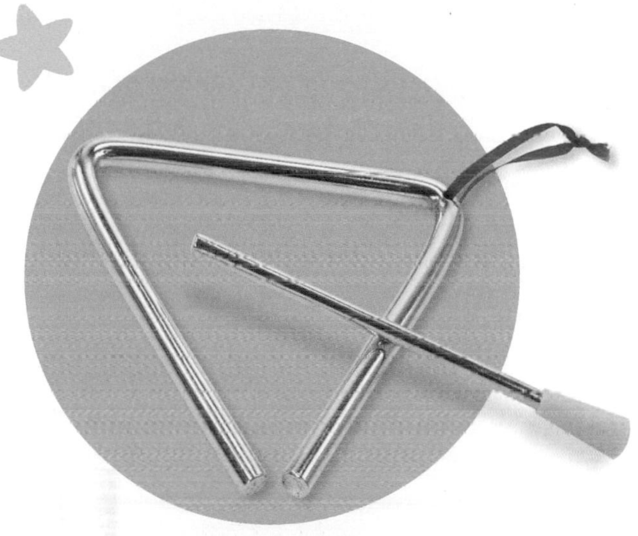

triangle

playing the triangle

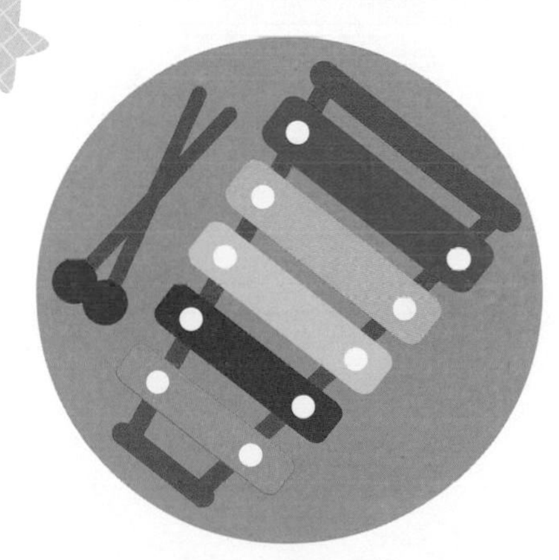

xylophone

playing the piano

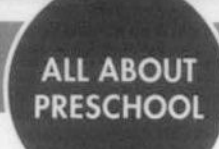

Home time

Circle the things you can take home from preschool.
Cross out the things you leave at preschool.

art

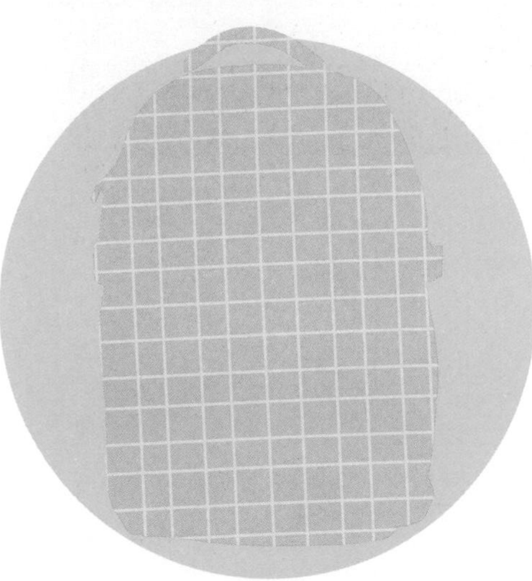

backpack

table

water bottle

coat

lunch box

teacher

Congratulations!

GOOD WORK AWARD!

Name: ....

has successfully completed the

Get Ready for **Pre-K** Jumbo Workbook

Date: ....

Search this page for the stickers you need.
TRACING
Pages 4–5
Pages 6–7
Pages 10–11
Pages 8–9
Pages 12–13
Pages 14–15
Pages 18–19
Pages 16–17
Pages 20–21
Extra stickers

Search this page for the stickers you need.
FIRST MAZES
Pages 22–23
Pages 24–25
Pages 26–27
Pages 28–29
Pages 30–31
Pages 32–33
Pages 34–35
Pages 36–37
Pages 38–39
Pages 40–41

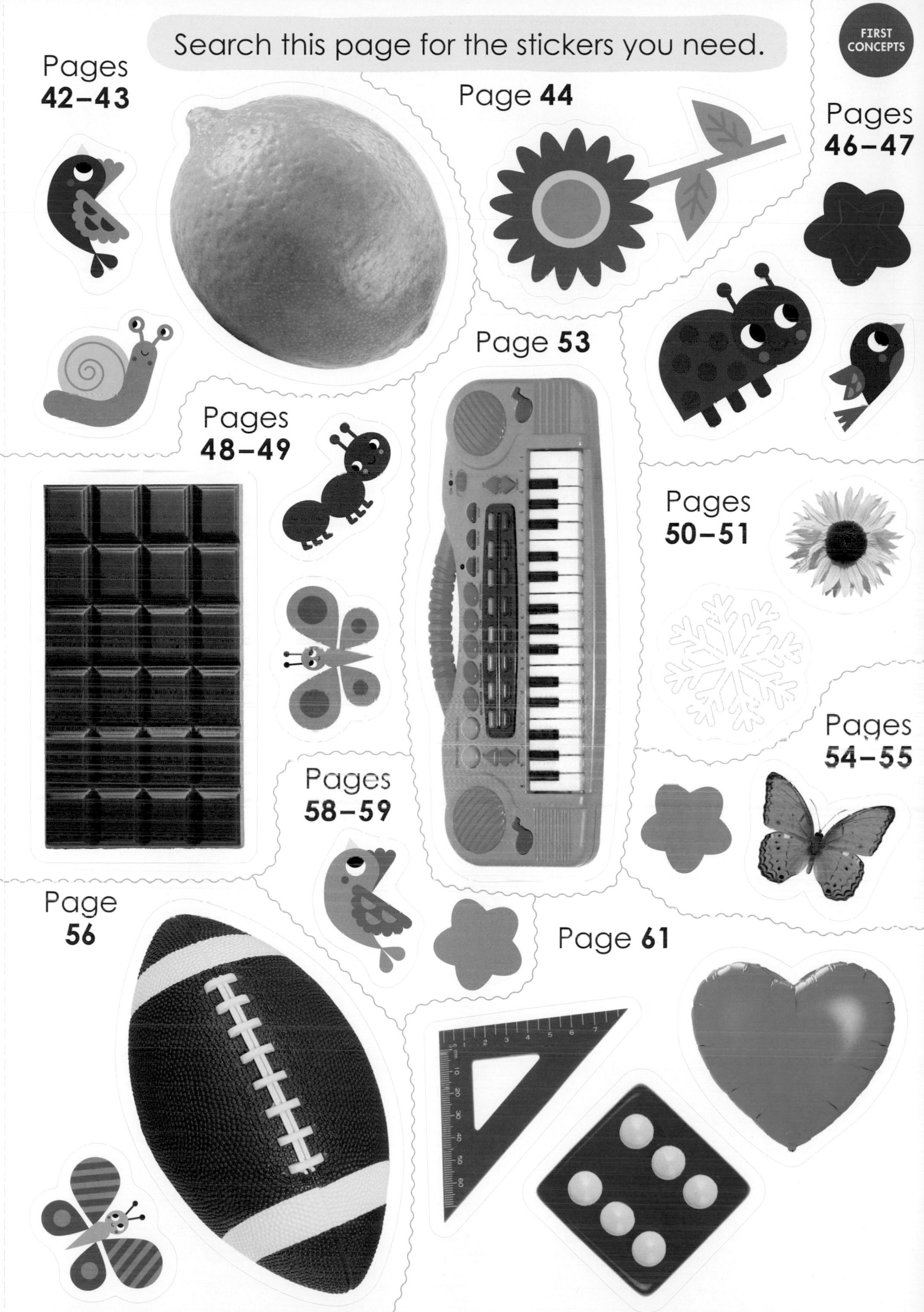

Search this page for the stickers you need.
FIRST CONCEPTS
Pages 42–43
Page 44
Pages 46–47
Page 53
Pages 48–49
Pages 50–51
Pages 54–55
Pages 58–59
Page 56
Page 61

Search this page for the stickers you need.
ABC
Pages 62–63
Pages 64–65
Pages 66–67
Pages 68–69
Pages 70–71
Pages 72–73
Pages 76–77
Pages 78–79
Pages 80–81
Pages 74–75
Page 82

Search this page for the stickers you need.
FIRST LETTER SOUNDS
Pages 84–85
Pages 86–87
Pages 88–89
Pages 90–91
Pages 92–93
Pages 94–95
Pages 96–97
Pages 98–99
Pages 102–103
Pages 100–101
Pages 104–105
Extra stickers

Search this page for the stickers you need.

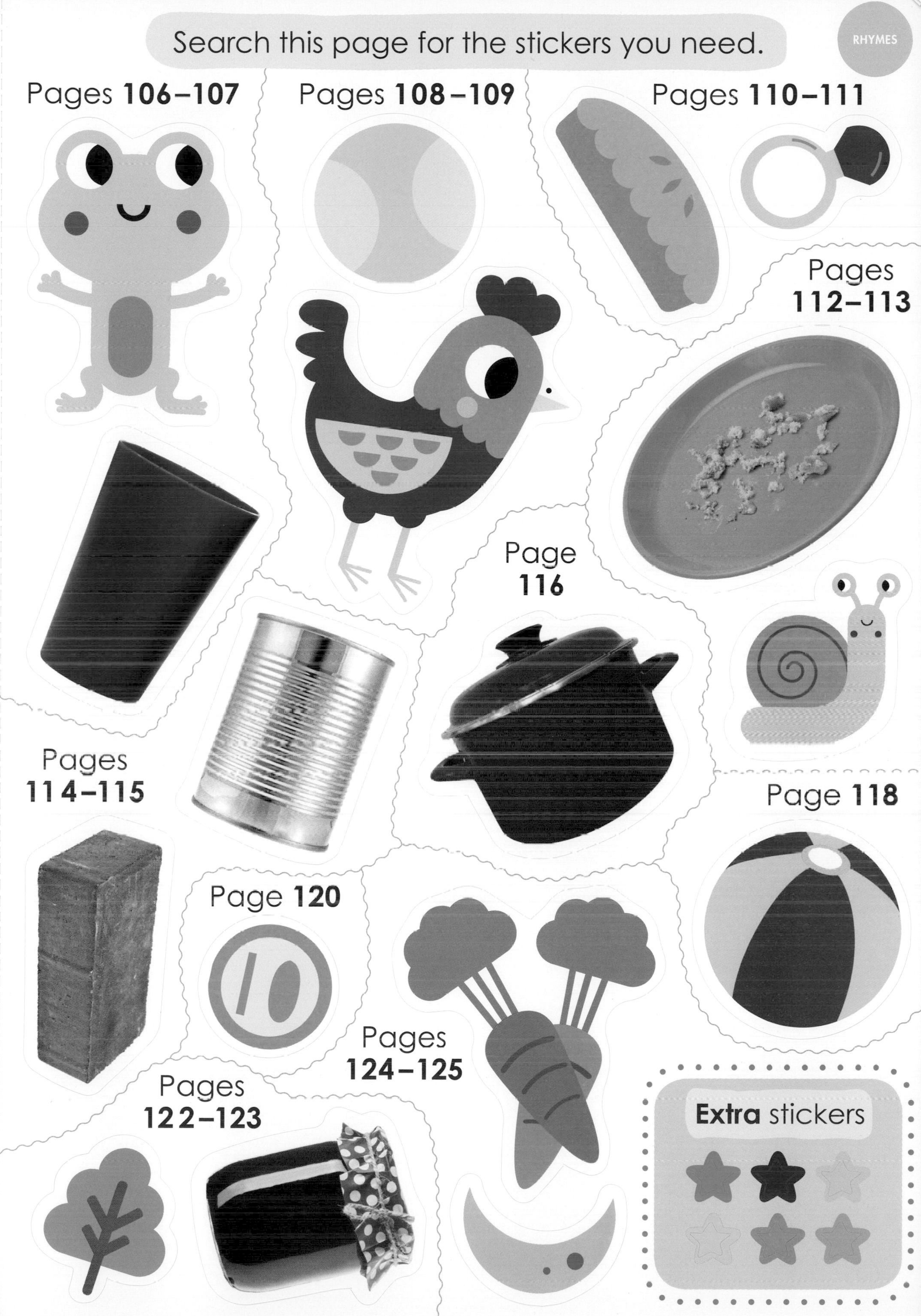

Search this page for the stickers you need.
HANDWRITING
Pages 126–127
Page 129
Page 130
Page 133
Page 135
Page 136
Page 139
Pages 140–141
Page 142
Pages 144–145
Page 147
Extra stickers

Search this page for the stickers you need.
COUNTING
Page 149
Page 151
Page 153
Page 157
Page 155
Page 159
Page 165
Page 161
Page 163
Page 167
Extra stickers

Search this page for the stickers you need.
SORTING
Pages 168–169
Page 171
Page 172
Pages 174–175
Pages 176–177
Page 178
Page 181
Extra stickers
Page 185
Pages 182–183

Search this page for the stickers you need.
VERY FIRST SCIENCE
Pages 186–187
1
2
3
1
2
3
Page 190
Page 193
Pages 188–189
Page 194
spring
fall
Pages 196–197
winter
summer
Page 199
Page 200
Pages 202–203
Extra stickers

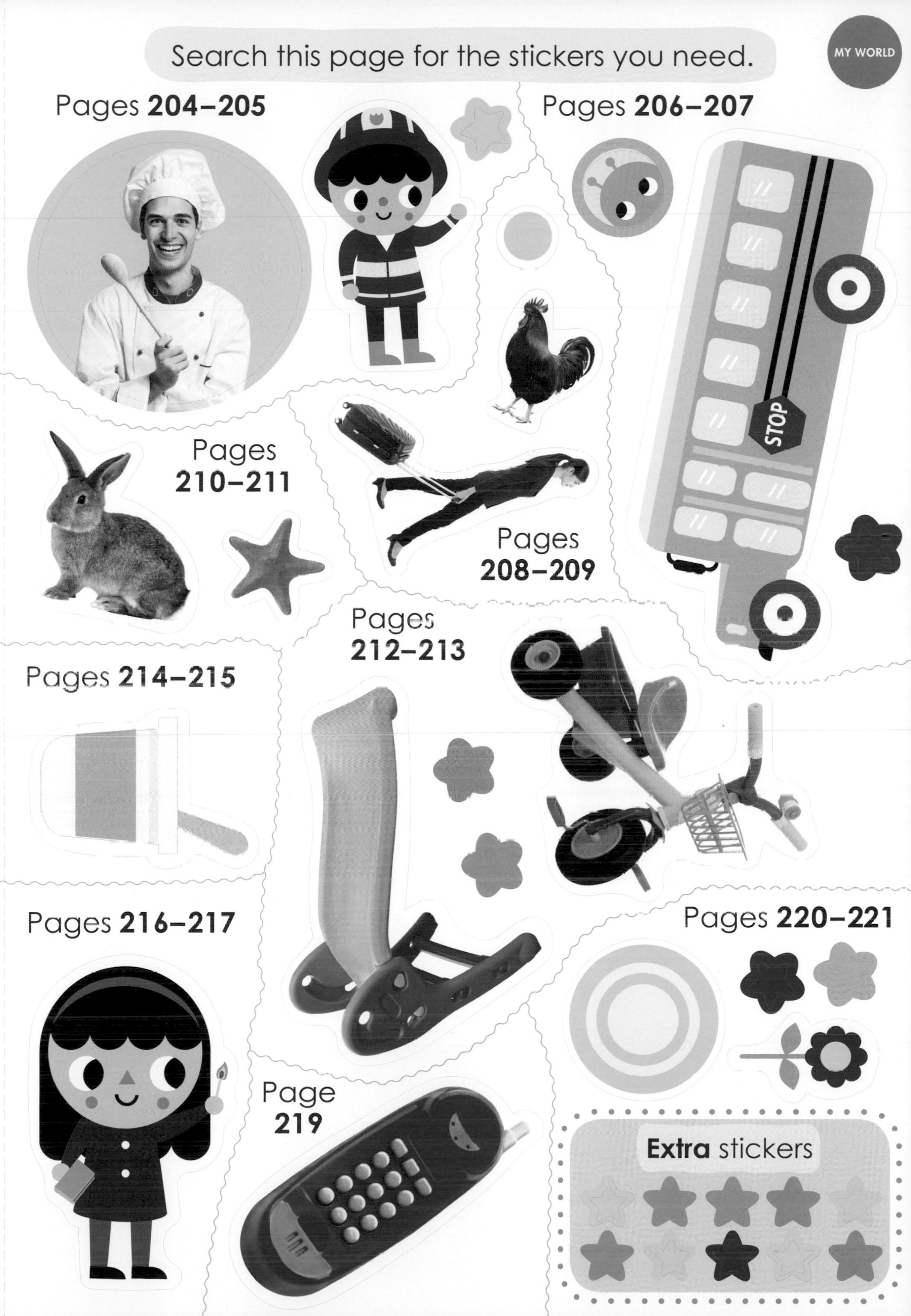
Search this page for the stickers you need.
MY WORLD
Pages 204–205
Pages 206–207
STOP
Pages 210–211
Pages 208–209
Pages 212–213
Pages 214–215
Pages 216–217
Pages 220–221
Page 219
Extra stickers

Search this page for the stickers you need.
ALL ABOUT PRESCHOOL
Pages 222–223
Pages 224–225
Page 228
Page 226
Pages 234–235
Page 232
Page 231
Pages 236–237
Pages 238–239
Certificate stickers